Passing it On

Folklore of St. Louis

Its Traditions, Superstitions, Rituals, and Folk Beliefs

John L. Oldani, PhD

2ND Edition, Revised & Updated

This one's for MOUSE,

whose legacy of true,

unconditional love underscored the virtues and value of our family lore.

She helped us to remember the good and to remind us what is

important.

She will be missed but never forgotten.

Reedy Press
PO Box 5131
St. Louis, MO 63139, USA

Library of Congress Control Number: 2012949158

ISBN: 978-1-935806-35-6

For more information, visit www.mysa.org and www.soccermadeinstlouis.com.

Please visit our website at www.reedypress.com.

Cover design by Alvin Zamudio

Photographs provided by Jim Wolf and the author.

Printed in the United States of America
12 13 14 15 16   5 4 3 2 1

CONTENTS

Acknowledgments   vii

Preface   xi

Introduction   xiii

Chapter 1   Folk Vocabulary and Sayings   3

Chapter 2   The Autograph Book Verse   12

Chapter 3   The Rhymes of Kids   26

Chapter 4   Riddles and Jokes   51

Chapter 5   Momisms   59

Chapter 6   Superstitions   67

Chapter 7   Holiday Lore   83

Chapter 8   Family Lore   93

Chapter 9   St. Louis Folk Foods   105

Chapter 10   Ethnic St. Louis Folklore   123

Chapter 11   Another Ethnicity   136

Chapter 12   Graffiti   146

Chapter 13   A Case Study of a St. Louis Family   165

Chapter 14   The Power of the Arch   176

Conclusion   180

About the Author   183

Index   184

ACKNOWLEDGMENTS

THERE'S A PROVERB OFTEN HEARD IN ST. LOUIS WHICH APPROPRIATELY AND coincidentally reflects the effect of this book on St. Louis lore: No one can whistle a symphony; it takes an orchestra to play it. The first edition of *Passing It On*, published in 2008, was the result of decades of folklore fieldwork and assembled from more than 100,000 folk texts. In the four short years since its release I have received hundreds of examples of folklore from and about the St. Louis region. The "folk" who frequently told me they had no folklore discovered in reading the first edition that vocabulary, rhymes, traditions, beliefs, superstitions, vocabulary, food, even family lore has, indeed, been part of their maturation. And they remembered and introduced themselves to their grandparents again. Together, they all played in the symphony.

To these new informants who eagerly sent me lore from their culture and "unlearned learning process," I am very grateful. You are too many to mention by name, but you will see your work in the specific chapter of your contribution. Some "folk" took the extra step and sent the actual artifact to me—autograph books, yearbooks, school papers, even family histories. These were valuable as context and validation.

Thanks, too, to all the St. Louis television and radio stations who invited me to appear and discuss the folklore of St. Louis. Many listeners responded with folklore examples that were new to my research but representative of St. Louis. The discussions were lively, educational, and fun.

Many organizations, also—church clubs, senior citizen groups, retirement homes, fraternal, civic, and social organizations—from all over the region and state, invited me to speak on folklore and its ap-plications. Their enthusiasm was contagious. So much material was collected at the meetings/discussions, it was difficult to record all of it. But it got done!

A special thanks to students from elementary through college who happily collected more examples of their vocabulary. Their "language" is clever, reflective, integrative, and lively. They are a creative and "hip" group who "really get it." Most importantly, I was able to collect it before it changes, and it will! But when it does, it will be possible to make comparisons and give some understanding to our current culture.

Perhaps more popular than any other folk text, however, were the pronouncements of MOM! Everyone, and I mean *everyone*, could identify with the "instructions" from "dear old mom." Many, many more have been added to this edition, and I still heard the phrase, "OMG, I've become my mother!" Rarely did people remember the advice from dad, and even dad, himself, often spoke of his wife as mom when he gave me examples! And so many St. Louisans sent me the same expressions! Is there only ONE St. Louis MOM? You decide.

As I said, it takes an orchestra. This new edition represents that orchestra. I am very, very grateful to all the informants.

A special thanks to the "boys" at Reedy Press, Josh Stevens and Matt Heidenry. They are truly the clichéd, "class act!" In fact, it was their idea to release this second edition. Their refreshing insights from the laymen's perspective about folklore were critical in explaining the "meaning" of lore. After many discussions and arguments, made civil by St. Louis donuts (which I bought every time!), *they* saw the light! I am fortunate to be associated with Josh and Matt. What they are doing and have done with Reedy Press is remarkable and an enormous contribution to St. Louis.

Thanks, again, to my wife, Carollee, who honored the "do not disturb" sign on my office door except to call me for meals! She patiently listened to my frustrations and let me rant! To my kids, Matt, Susan Hendrickson, and David, their spouses, Jennifer, Joe, and Monica, and my grandkids, Gemma, Josie, Ceci, Charlie, and Gianna who served, again, as my guinea pigs listening to my newly collected lore, I truly appreciate your support. Micki Bisesi, my sister, was an appropriate nag in repeatedly asking about the book. She is my best agent! Throughout the writing and collecting, I have never forgotten who started all this for me. My parents, Charlie and Mary Knez Oldani, were careful in keeping our family traditions, not just in the practice of them, but in explaining what the lore meant. They are missed every day. Grandma Cecilia Knez remains the spirit throughout all the lore!

PREFACE
READERS BECAME INFORMANTS

ALL THAT I DESCRIBED IN THE INTRODUCTION TO THE FIRST EDITION OF *Passing It On* still relates. In fact, it is more relevant than ever! Often, in my research over the past several decades, it was necessary to explain to people (known as informants) what is meant by "folklore." Most people think that it means old wives' tales or untruths, silly information, or even another form of trivia. After the explanation, some still don't' get it and tell me that they don't have any folklore in their lives. Of course, this is not true. Folklore is the unlearned learning process off of us undergo every day.

When *Passing It On* was released in 2008, readers were introduced to a new way of understanding their culture, especially the culture of St. Louis. What followed was very welcome and bordering on incredible. People from all over the region became "informants." Those who believed they had NO folklore suddenly remembered. The examples of the lore in the first edition sparked their memories of their own experiences and learning. I received hundreds, even thousands, more of examples of St. Louis folklore. The common response with their new information was usually, "I didn't know that was folklore. I could have given you some examples for the book." Well, now they have, and I am grateful.

What are included in this revised edition are the basic folk texts in the study of a region or culture. Since the word is the basic text for all of the oral traditions of folklore, I have added many examples of folk vocabulary. In the first edition I did not list the hundreds of slang words from the metropolitan area. Readers let me know about it and send me example after example, some of which is very, very good, but cannot be put to print! I'm sure you've heard them expressed. This edition gives examples of St. Louis slang that is heard "on the street" and carries meanings directed related to their pronunciation or sounds.

Their currency is revealing and educational for all of us. Check and see how many of the words or phrases you know or have used. You are "passing it on."

"Momisms," those "threats" from our mothers received the most response from readers of the first edition. I believe that mothers all read the same "mothers' bible," as the pronouncements recognized by a variety of folk groups. Somehow, mothers have passed on their cautionary, threatening, moralistic sayings to all children, not just their own! I have included more of these "MOMISMS" in this revised edition. You will notice your mother or grandmother, again, and I hope reflect.

Again, as I have said repeatedly, all the lore presented in this new edition is not exhaustive. Far from it! There is lore in everything. Collecting and documenting the different folk texts is necessary to understand ourselves and our culture. If it is not collected and preserved, it will be lost forever and a vital part of our character studies will be gone. It is not an easy task. Readers of the first edition became willing informants. This new edition of one more attempt to apply the functions of folklore: validation, education, compensation, and bonding, to the St. Louis region. After reading this, you will have more examples, I am certain. Preserve them as they define you and continue to pass them on! In fact, I can preserve them: stlouisfolklore.com. Thanks to all of you for your folklore and willingness to share with others. I am certain many of you met your grandparents again!

INTRODUCTION
YOUR GRANDMOTHER'S EDUCATION

It all started with my maternal grandmother, Cecilia Karlic Knez, an immigrant from Croatia. She was born in 1884, died in 1983, and was the carrier of folklore for almost one hundred years. Leaving her large family, her possessions, her friends, her very life behind, widowed and seeking a better life, she arrived at Ellis Island in 1912. And when she "met" me in 1942, my life was forever changed.

Her home, friends, activities, and possessions may have been left on the shores of the Adriatic, but she brought with her the classic oral traditions of her culture. She became our *griot*—the oral historian—from whom I not only learned the meaning of tradition, culture, and family, but also, through her stories, proverbs, expressions, beliefs, superstitions, and even food, I learned much more. I learned compassion, empathy, trust, respect, logic, spirituality, confidence, courage, character, competence, and, most of all, how to laugh.

It was easy listening to her ghost stories, those supernatural events that actually "happened to her." It was educational to hear her Croatian-spoken aphorisms: "Bide your time and when you catch him sleeping, pour hot lead in his ear!" The translation is not as poetic as the original, but the meaning is just as clear. Later on I would hear, "What goes around comes around"; or "Every dog has his day"; or "Don't get mad, get even"; or "Don't wrestle with a pig, you only get dirty and the pig loves it!" The American meanings are many and can be applied in a variety of situations, but hers were very specific.

I learned about black cats, and opened umbrellas in a house, a hat on the bed, what a birthmark meant, and what a caul was. I learned about Fat Tuesday and fritij; about the gift of folk songs and folk dances; how egg shells fertilize a garden and Epsom salts can give roses strong roots; how *pelinkovac* (plum brandy) can cure anything; what a full moon meant, or a red sunrise, or a ring around the moon; or the medicinal qualities of onions, potatoes, or garlic; how to "scapegoat"; cures for colic, freckles, boils, and sties; and how to make bread without a recipe or *potica* simply from tradition.

The author's grandmother, Cecilia Karlic Knez, and a young admirer.

And, by the way, through all those years I was learning how to diagram a sentence, work an algebraic equation, memorize conjugations, and "calculate" in calculus. Since I left my formal education, I have not been asked to do any of these things! But I have been asked numerous times in conversation, about my superstitions my own wedding traditions, the pattern of my family celebrations, to remember an autograph book verse, a folk game or folk song, a Halloween tradition, or a folk cure. I have been asked about my folklore, my informal learning process. And I understood that the very informal methodology of education was indelible and explained a lot about my culture and the American culture. There was the optimism of the wedding lore; the thinking process of kick the can or step ball; the socialization of children's jeers; the education involved in proverbs; the concept of teamwork in hopscotch or Red Rover; the values of "momisms"; the tradition of autograph book verses; the freedom in graffiti but also the loneliness; the competitive urges of conundrums, riddles, or jokes; the maturation of children in parodies of "sacred texts"; the expected rebellion in searching for an identity in jump-rope rhymes; the recognition of a future norm in "Mother May I"; the testing of parental control in insults; the need for order in counting-out rhymes.

In these ways and countless others, the lore of a society is based on the oral tradition that groups of "folk" pass along whether kids, teenagers, adults, quilters, fraternities, religious groups, ethnic, racial, or gender folk. Wherever rites of passage are integral to the culture, there is the lore. Wherever the character of a culture lies—however it is defined—there is a lore. And each group within a "folk" attempts to explain the world to themselves, to rationalize, relate, cooperate, stamp an identity, and achieve an independence. All are reflected in the oral traditions of folklore. And every one of us has been touched by it and may have survived because of it.

All this lore, I later understood in higher academic settings, can be used to explain much of a society's cultural characteristics. The difference in national cultural groups on a global level and the difference between generational groups on a micro level can be explained through folklore.

For the first two decades of my life I had listened to the oral history of Croatia tempered by the American experience of my grandmother. I learned how she, and her folk group, applied the oral traditions of their "old country" to the young culture of the United States. A new lore was developing, but it was based on a standard formula and some very similar themes. Its study became my academic mission. How has the lore, transmitted in a migratory oral, traditional, anonymous way, defined America?

My PhD in American Studies resulted from twenty years of listening, gathering, and recording. As a professor of American Studies I established a Folklore Archive in which the oral traditions from the St. Louis region are collected, catalogued, and researched for patterns and traits. The spoken word, proverb, aphorism, joke, riddle, expression, holiday traditions, birth lore, death rituals, wedding and birth rituals, customs, folk songs, folk art, folk music, folk parody, children's lore in jump ropes, games, autograph book verses, folk foods, superstitions, historical lore, academic lore, school lore—wherever the folk group, there was the lore that bound it. Eventually almost 100,000 items or texts were collected from the St. Louis region representing the lore of each folk group. And it was the root of their identity.

For twenty-five years I had a program on KMOX Radio (CBS) in St. Louis, where for an hour each week people would call in with their lore. And so I collected more examples or validated what had been previously identified. Callers from around the country would respond with their version of the same folk genre. People were reliving and remembering that oral tradition that defined their lives and that was not learned in a formal educational setting.

My other call-in radio programs in Boston, Los Angeles, Phoenix, and Chicago gathered more lore that, again, gave other versions of similar St. Louis lore, always with a slight difference. Finally, the legendary Johnny Cash and I collaborated on a radio program to establish the importance of lore in the lives of all of us. The innocent games we played as kids or the traditions we practiced at our weddings or the jokes we told as kids and then as adults—all these examples and more reflect more of us than any other cultural device.

All of this is a serious academic study. For hundreds of years folk stories, legends, and tales have been collected by scholars in many countries. Variants of the lore are given a systematic type, a catalogue number, documentation to source, and a comparison to different cultures. A science of fieldwork developed within such academic areas as anthropology, sociology, or interdisciplinary studies. Archives of folklore collections catalogued by type, region, ethnicity, or many other categories, were established and are made available to serious research-ers of a country's culture. Prestigious universities, including many American ones, offer degrees from the associate through the PhD in the science of folklore.

So what is folklore exactly? First, it is oral in its transmission. One person tells another and then that person tells another and so on. The joke, the expression, or the ritual becomes a custom. And no one really knows where it started. So anonymity is another criterion. In attempting to understand the world, all folk groups learn to explain occurrences or rationalize events.

A third criterion is that the lore is always passed along in a tradi-tional way. For example, young girls have been jumping rope on grade-school playgrounds for decades and jump rope is still very popular. But the verses of 2008 are far different from the verses of 1950. None of the rhymes was learned in a formal educational setting, but rather by tra-dition. Always the themes are important to the girls doing the jumping and reflect their concerns about life which they don't fully understand. Jumping and chanting in a prescribed cadence add a sense of play.

Often the same folk expression, saying, or verse is found in an-other region, and a fourth criterion, the existence of different versions, suggests even more strongly the need to express oneself exactly as the immediate culture demands. For example, someone in one region might believe that a black cat crossing his or her path is bad luck. Someone in another area knows the same belief, but has learned that spitting in the direction of the black cat and then continuing neutralizes the bad luck. Little does the second person know that his belief goes back to the ancients, who thought that spitting sends our "soul spirits" to create good luck. The belief continues—again, without formal education— but the practice is repeated over and over again. Black cats, as symbols of bad luck, are the theme; the belief is still there; but the optimism of some Americans can convert that bad luck. And observers of the American character have often said that optimism defines us. Found in the folk texts? Absolutely!

St. Louis is one of those regions with a distinct lore. What serve as the basic folklore examples heard and used in the area may be heard in all parts of the country and even elsewhere in the world. But the spin on the folk text and its delivery become characteristically St. Louis's.

Every one of us has been touched by lore. It is integral to our personality and our world view. It serves as our history, our past, our future, our fears, our triumphs, our maturation, our generational ages, our very character.

Folklore can be a chance to reconnect with our grandparents, parents, and siblings to relive our traditions or family history; to understand our contemporaries or colleagues better; and to make connections in this age of very complex changes.

I have been aware of the many forms of folklore and studied them for more than thirty years, and I hear and see new things every day. Folklore has helped explain my world for decades.

Say hello to yourself in each of the succeeding chapters, which are by no means exhaustive. I hope you will recognize where you were, what you were doing, why you did it, and why you still do it. I hope you will learn some new lore to help explain this complex, changing world. And I hope, most of all, that you continue your traditional lore. It's the one treasure that must not be lost in our "throwaway" society.

Grandma 'Cela would be grateful!

PASSING IT ON

CHAPTER 1

FOLK VOCABULARY AND SAYINGS

FROM "SCRUBBY DUTCH" TO HIGHWAY "FARTY"

THE BASIS OF ALL FOLKLORE COLLECTING AND RESEARCH IS THE SIMPLE word. Often a single word can identify a region, and sometimes the word is used in a phrase that also is peculiar to a region. Either way, the texts that exist in different areas become indelible to the character of the region and often define the culture.

St. Louis is made up of many different neighborhoods that have changed demographics over the years, but the lore of the language still has a grip on some remaining families or in the memories and speech patterns of those who have moved. The vocabulary and expressions become historically important, reflective of a culture, and characteristically identified with St. Louis. The evidence is still being collected decades after it was first heard.

Since the publication of the first *Passing It On* book, informants from all over St. Louis have sent me examples of folk vocabulary specific to their neighborhood, family, or folk group. The words, phrases, or sayings are used in the purist folklore sense of bonding, validating, educating, or compensating for an event or occurrence. They help fill the gap when an occasion requires folk expressions.

Sometimes the expressions are only familial and known specifically to that group but are transmitted to friends and become part of the larger, regional use. Some words are manufactured in a folk group to "fit the need." They survive through remembrance and use and are resurrected when the group occasionally meets. Other folk terms might be derivative of the current popular culture, slang terms, or slurs related to an outside group or person. All have a purpose and meaning and help define the place where they are used.

The following examples of folk vocabulary fall under all categories and functions of folklore. Perhaps you've used them or heard them and passed them on to friends where the words have taken on a new life. Many, you will note, are slang and created by the culture. These were collected in the past five years but have been used by folk groups for many more years.

FOLK WORDS, PRONUNCIATION, AND GRAMMAR

The term "Scrubby Dutch" is still used, as it has been for decades, to describe the influence of the German immigrants to St. Louis. Widely known for their cleanliness, St. Louisans of German heritage swept alleys, ironed everything, and cleaned on a religious schedule. The most famous cleaning task was scrubbing the "stoop" in front of the house. Concrete steps were brushed clean every Saturday and still are today. Thrift, discipline, and a strong work ethic are traits reflective of this culture. There is even a neighborhood in the southern part of St. Louis City known as Dutchtown.

- Clothes and dishes are "warshed." And both are "rinched" after "warshing." The dishes are put in the "zink."
- Breakfast treats for Sundays are still "panny-cakes."
- Dragonflies are snake doctors, witch doctors, or darning needles.
- A soda is a "sodie," not a "pop."
- A donut is a "cruller" no matter what its shape or filling.
- People's hearts "tump and tump."
- "Wampus kitty" is used in place of a scavenger hunt or a snipe hunt.
- But "catty wampus" is when things are all confused.

- A "concrete" is a very thick shake or malt and sometimes synonymous with a "blizzard." Ted Drewes Custard in St. Louis probably coined the term, but its application is widely used.

- A "brown cow" is a drink made with vanilla ice cream and root beer. An "orange cow" uses orange Whistle soda and vanilla ice cream. A "red cow" uses Vess Cream Soda and vanilla ice cream. A "black cow" uses Pepsi-Cola or Coca-Cola and ice cream.

- "Down by the Gravois (grav-oy)" is used for directions related first to a streetcar and later to a shopping district; both reference a major thoroughfare in the city.

- Goethe, a street in South St. Louis City, is pronounced, "go-thee," not "gur-ta" like the famous playwright and philosopher who gave his name to the street.

- St. Louisans usually use the "s" for their neighbors to the east: Illi-noise!

- "Anthat" is used for etcetera: "We helped them move their furniture anthat."

- "Go by" is a commonly used expression: "Go by the store and get some bread."

- People "come by" money when they receive unexpected cash.

- "Grunty" is euphemistic for a bowel movement.

- The major thoroughfare in St. Louis is Highway 40, pronounced "farty."

- "Sundy" is either a day of the week or an ice cream treat.

- Leftovers for dinner are called "mustgo." Everything in the refrigerator must go!

- There is no such thing as DUCT tape. It is always DUCK tape.

- Sometimes St. Louisans have to change their "winchell" wipers.

- St. Louis homeowners don't have a refrigerator; they have an "ice box."

- There are no "couch" potatoes in St. Louis. A couch or sofa is a "divan."

- Tennis shoes, jogging shoes, running shoes—whatever—all are called "sneakers."

- Some St. Louisans cook on a "skillet" and not a frying pan, and some fry in a "spider" rather than a frying pan.

- When things in the house are really messy and someone notices they might say, "Things are all over the hurricane deck."

- A "blind fish" is a popular name given to food eaten by Catholics during Lent. Fish is a very popular food during the weeks before Easter, and church fish fries are even becoming a folk custom. But when some St. Louisans got tired of eating fish and knew that meat was not allowed, they would prepare eggs or French toast or pancakes and call it "blind fish."

- Some people use the term "snap beans" for any kind of green bean.

- "Go on with your rat killin'" is a popular expression when someone is very busy and can't stop to talk on the phone and interrupt his or her work. "Go on with your rat killin' and I'll talk to you later," you say as you walk away.

- A biscuit is referred to as a "dodger." The word is often used in an expression of acceptance. When someone is invited to another's house for a party, a dinner, or any kind of celebration, they could simply accept graciously. But in some parts of St. Louis the reply is usually, "I'll sop up my dodger in your soup anytime." There has to be a folk poetry in the acceptance. These expressions eventually take on a folk life.

- "Dunch," Bunch," "Lupper," or "Blinner," are combined words for meals of the day. If it's too late for breakfast, for example, and past lunch, a person can have a "blinner." Some folk believe that men use the phrases because they are too macho for words like brunch!

- "Sassy Tuna" refers to a young adult, female flirt.

- An "ace" is a person's best friend.

- A "sookie" is a cookie drenched in milk (not a character on *True Blood*).

- When a person "snurfs" he is burping and sneezing at the same time. But a burp and a hiccup is a "biccup."

- When a person develops the layer of hanging fat under her arm it is known as "bingo wings," from the "blue hair" set who play bingo all the time.

- "Musquirt and mustard snot" relate to the watery substance from the first squeeze of the mustard jar and the dry stuff that remains on the life of the bottle. When some mustard oozes out of the sandwich and remains dried on your finger, it is called "musticle." But "farge" is the dry stuff around the ketchup bottle.

- Flip flops are "Jesus sneakers."

- A person who wears only name brands is a "label whore."

- Spending too much time at the mall can give you "mallitis."

- When you open a can of soda (or pop) and it fizzes, it's a "coka soaka."

- An elderly man who wears a Speedo to a beach is a "grape smuggler."

- If you ask a person if he has any "friends" you are asking for cigarettes. This is a clever cover up for the person who feels abused because he smokes.

- When someone does something gawky or weird he is "pulling a Neil."

- When a person has to attend to some "paperwork" he is going to the bathroom.

- "Compstipation" is when you can't get online on your computer.

- When barbeque sauce remains on your face it's "beardbeque."

- An "Aberzombie" wears only designer label clothes. The same person may be said to have "fallen into a GAP."

- When a person has a "bert" he has a unibrow . . . named about Bert on *Sesame Street*?

- Too thick eyebrows? You have "eyebrellas."

- A "puck bunny" is a groupie of hockey players.

- When there are more men than ladies at a gathering it's called a "sausage party."

- When someone is in trouble through his own fault, he "stuck his fork in the toaster."

- When a young lady shows parts of her body while bending over, it's called a "happy birthday."

- Women who attach a string or band to their glasses have "canasta glasses."

- Waitresses call poor tippers "chicken feeders."

- A man who speaks to people with smarmy, soft, flattering words is a "Hallmark tongue."

- Certain fast restaurants are called "Choke and Puke" places.

- When someone is "out of the cupboard," he admits he is a Harry Potter fan.

- When two guys fight and eventually split over the same girl, it's a "dudevorce."

- A "toilet mummy" is an excessively clean person who puts toilet tissue all over a public toilet seat.

- "Ghost taste" is that awful feeling after a burp.

- A "flubby" is a wrinkle in the wall-to-wall carpet.

- A teenage girl who is very popular but very controlling is called "Heather."

- If a thing or person is beyond "cool" it is "frozen."

- When you have to sneeze and you can't, you have a "Leroy."

- When you recognize someone ahead of you, you "backonize" them.

- Tell someone after they thank you for something: "PIAM: The pleasure is all mine."

- An "Amway Christian" is one who believes that wealth is a gift from Jesus and should be pursued.

- When planning shopping or traveling at certain times, one must consider the "SCF: Senior Citizen Factor."

- When the conversation is alien to you, you can remark, "That's a 747," meaning it's over your head.

- When a lady has "love handles" she also has a "side ass."

- When you forget something you might have "brain fade," "brain cramp," or "brain freeze."

- Acne on your back or shoulders? It's called "backne."

- A person who "always" has problems and talks about them is an "emotional vampire."

- After Thanksgiving dinner, for example, many people have a "food coma" from eating too much.

- You have to "chilax"—chill out and relax.

- "It's about as useful as a chocolate teapot." Could also apply to a person!

- A "lung cookie" is what develops the morning after a big night of drinking.

- A person who is really disliked is an "ankle," because he is "lower than an asshole."

- A very thin girl is sometimes knows as "Ally McHurl," from the television program.

- When a person is really obnoxious he is on or above the "ABS: Asshole behavior scale."

- A "cubicle coma" is when work, especially on a Monday, causes total exhaustion.

- When a person wants a "Facebook minute," she wants some undetermined time. (Social media has entered the vocabulary because friends of Facebook spend so much time looking at their friends that time gets away from them.)

- An "airbiscuit" is a polite term for passing gas.

- When a person yawns and displays some spittle, he just did a "cobra yawn."

- When Friday night rolls around and the work load is over, it's time to "moon the dog." It's time to go out and have a great time.

- When a person says something silly, stupid, or obvious, "You're a Mensa candidate."

- The age of a longtime smoker, whose face shows the effect of smoking, is gauged by "nicotime."

- When a driver, usually at rush hour, tries to get ahead in a long line of cars, he is doing "auto ballet."

- "Drupple" is that stuff around your mouth when you wake up.

- A good-looking clerk at a fast food restaurant is a "McGirl."

- A "moon pig" is a chunky person who spends too much time indoors and then tries to get tan in one day.

- A male companion who is dull or not handsome is called a "Marlon Blando."

- "Cheappuchinno" is the "special" flavors of coffee from a convenience store.

- A lady who is always involved in others' business is a "Jackie Horner," from the thumb in the nursery rhyme.

- "Gleek" is the spittle from a person who is talking to you.

- When the ladies' restroom has a long line, one might opt, if really necessary, to "commode commando" and use the men's room.

- When a corporate manager really wants his department to achieve a goal, he asks them to "burn the tambourines." This can apply to an endeavor when a person wants to work hard to achieve a goal.

- Power point presentations are "required" in corporate America and at large conventions. But the jargon is often overused, and participants sarcastically refer to it as "bulls**t bingo."

- Computer technicians often get "DUQ: Dumb User Question."

- A person who talks too much, to the point of babbling, took a "mental laxative."

- Any controlling person can be said to believe they have a "Barney Fifedom," where nothing is accomplished.

- When a person has to rise early, he gets up at "the Amish ass crack of dawn," which is very early.

- When you can't think of a word, which is on the "tip of your tongue," you just had an "onion."

- When you are "shappy" you are shocked and happy at the same time, like winning the lottery.

- When a person seems to have all the pat answers she is speaking in "Oprahisms."

- A man with large, sagging breasts has "breasticles."

- "You worry about everything. Don't frustulate."

- The most annoying person you know is a "nargle."

- A woman who "controls" her male companion is a "Nancy Neuter."

The basic root of all folk texts is the word. St. Louis lore, as in many regions of the country, has its own distinct vocabulary, pronunciation, and even grammar. But these "words" can lead to complex folk traditions in legends, superstitions, or even proverbs. And they always help to define a region. But only the natives can say St. Louie! Visitors need to show more respect!

CHAPTER 2

THE AUTOGRAPH BOOK VERSE
YOURS TIL THE ARCH FALLS!

NOSTALGIA IS "IN!" IT'S ALWAYS BEEN FUN TO REMEMBER THE PAST, THE "good old days" when the grass was always greener, and the cold was always colder, and the summers were always more carefree, casual, and spontaneous. But in this age of information circling around the Internet and rapid complex changes, coined as "raplexity," the need to "stop the world and get off" for a breather has never been more real.

Grade school and high school reunions have become businesses in themselves. They are even advertised in newspapers, invitations are sent via the Internet, and, not surprisingly, there are "find your former classmates" websites. The overwhelming pace of change has created a real hunger for a past, an identity, a sense of belonging—a desire to be "planted" somewhere!

Reliving the past has always been important to Americans, but its pervasiveness has taken on cosmic significance. Our society has become so mobile: moving, changing jobs, new family structures, workforce applications, corporate mergers—all have contributed to our sense of living with no attachments. Perhaps more than any other trait, Americans need to be rooted.

The reunions may be held every five or ten years or only on the "significant" twenty-five- or fifty-year dates. Some classmates may have kept in contact with each other, but for the greater majority, the special gatherings allow an opportunity to relive the past, compare school stories, remembrances, and idiosyncrasies, and catch up on the latest news about classmates. Reunions define an important part of the American character.

Arguably, more than any other city in the United States, and perhaps the world, St. Louis craves roots, identity, connections, and affiliation. The most popular question, which has taken on folklore proportions, is: WHERE DID YOU GO TO HIGH SCHOOL? It is the starter to many conversations with strangers—and those from another city who are greeted for the first time with that question may actually question the motive of the questioner. Sometimes used as a "come-on" line in a bar, the question helps to create lasting friendships and can lead to more innocent intimacy and a strong connection. At least two books have been written with this very St. Louis question as the title!

But a second folklore text is also important in the lives of St. Louisans: autograph books. They are not a St. Louis invention, to be sure, but they are used extensively, and their contents seem to be more varied than in other parts of the United States. At the artifacts table at every reunion, the autograph book is the most popular item. It is the one item that is saved by more people than any other remembrance of grammar school or high school.

More importantly, in our dizzying pace of change, the autograph book stays constant. It never changes, and we can pick it up any time and remember. It is our personal history, our personal past, our personal memory keeper. "You know he's a dentist now; I could have married him!" Regret, affirmation, smugness, pride, loyalty—all is there in the autograph book.

Sometimes the books were leather bound, even with tufted leather and closed with a zipper. Sometimes they were fastened with a ribbon. Some were even lined. But almost all of them were small enough—four inches by six inches—to serve as the intimate and necessary past. For the pure folklore traditionalist they have become the primary sources for their personal history, no matter what life has dealt them.

The real folk texts were expressed in a variety of ways on the blank pages of the book. No one knows where the expressions were learned. Certainly there was no formal class about writing in autograph books. But the anonymity was erased only slightly by the signature of the folk who wrote it. And the meaning, although not always consistent with the character of the writer, spoke to a shared experience for eight or twelve years or to the importance of friendship or even to a sincere goodbye masked by an inconsistent silliness.

There are certain purposes in all autograph folk texts: Beware of the future adult life; beware of marriage; don't forget to do things the "right way"; and remember "me" always. It was often a mark of popularity, also, to get the most signatures and the most variety. But the most significant aspect was presentation of the message in a verse form. The creativity of the "folk" is very clearly seen in this genre. It was also more common for young ladies to express more sentimentality and young men to be "silly" to avoid the "mushiness" of saying goodbye. Yet everyone wrote in them, and later in yearbooks. This universal application speaks to the strong tradition of folklore defining a need.

Some St. Louis autograph book verses were collected from as far back as the nineteenth century, and the connotations have changed little.

FRIENDSHIP FOREVER: THE "YOURS TIL" FORMULA VERSE

- Yours til the moon stops shining
- Yours til Bob Burnes (a legendary St. Louis sports journalist)
- Yours til soda pops
- Yours til the Mississippi River wears rubber pants to keep its bottom dry
- Yours til Niagara falls
- Yours til vanilla wafers
- Yours til pillows bring their cases to court
- Yours til butter flies
- Yours til the moth bawls
- Your til lemon drops
- Yours til lip sticks

- Yours til the comic strips

- Yours til the boll weevil's problem is solved
  (Apparently this is an old verse in which the writer believed the solution
  was not possible. The expression was later used by the family to mean
  something that would last forever. This is reminiscent of the lore used by
  people from northern Italy who, when asked how long someone will need
  to do something, answer: "As long as the Duomo!" The Cathedral in Milan
  is cleaned every day and it takes one year from the start to get through the
  enormous Cathedral back to the place where the cleaning started!)

- Yours til the side walks

- Yours til France fries Turkey in Greece and eats it on China

- Yours til the undertaker takes you under

- Yours til the Jewel boxes.
  (Reference to a St. Louis landmark, the Jewel Box)

- Yours til Bud's wiser!

- Yours til St. Louis City and County merge!
  (A reference to the many municipalities surrounding the city of St. Louis
  and the many failed discussions and attempts over decades about merging all
  of them into one St. Louis City.)

- Yours til Highway 40 runs smoothly!
  (This decades-old verse is full of irony because an historical decision to
  close the major St. Louis thoroughfare for at least two years for repairs had
  been major news for more than a year—but the verse is much older. This
  shows the pervasiveness of the construction mentality in St. Louisans!)

- Yours til the kitchen sinks

- Yours til The Hill is not Italian!
  (The Hill is St. Louis's Italian neighborhood, nationally famous for its total
  ethnicity and not likely to change—ever.)

- Yours til the Veiled Prophet prophesies!
  (A famous St. Louis tradition is the Veiled Prophet, who visits "his" city
  every year for a parade, elaborate party for debutante introductions, and a
  large fair to celebrate. His identity is never disclosed, and a favorite pastime
  among some groups is to guess who is the privileged Prophet for the year.
  Others have protested his presence. Both groups help contribute to a pure
  St. Louis legend.)

ROSES ARE RED:
THE RHYMING FORMULA

Most of these verses follow the children's sing-song poetry learned as toddlers. The rhythmic meter is a familiar pattern that all can recognize, but the expressions, often with a twist and a silly insult, help to show the maturation of the writer. "Baby" rhymes are no longer part of their lore so they can parody it. Also, the fear of being too "mushy" and not being "cool" is expressed with a childish humor.

Roses are red
Violets are green
I think you're in love
With Mr. Clean. (1999)

Roses are red
Violets are blue
You've got a nose
Like a B-52!

Roses are red
Violets are blue
Pickles are sour
And so are you. (1954)

Roses are red
Violets are blue
Monkeys like you
Should be in the zoo. (1962)

Roses are red
Violets are blue
The whole world
Knows that I love you. (2002)
      (A direct recent verse signed by the writer; an indication of the changes in
      the freedom of expression over the years.)

Roses are red
And violets are blue
I love me
And you love you. (2003)

Roses are red
Violets are green
Take my advice
And use Listerine. (1987)

Roses are red
Violets are blue
Sugar is sweet
And so is syrup! (2004)
    (a purposely, discordant meta-folklore rhyme)

Roses are red
Violets are black
You'd look better
With a knife in your back. (2005)

Roses are red
Violets are green
You have a shape
Like a washing machine. (1977)

Roses are red
Violets are blue
Sugar is sweet
It's nothing like you. (1995)

The roses are wilted
The violets are dead
The sugar is lumpy
And so is your head. (2001)

Roses are red
Violets are blue
Garbage stinks
And so do you. (1960)

Roses are red
Violets are blue
Umbrellas get lost
Why don't you?

Roses are red
Violets are green
My face is funny
But yours is a scream. (1970)

Roses are green
Oranges are blue
If you had 5 drinks
You'd think so too.

Roses are red
Green is the vine
I wish your pajamas were next to mine
Now don't get excited and don't get so red
I mean on the clothesline not in my bed. (1951)
     (Seems risque for 1951!)

Roses are red
Violets are pink
Immediately after the 17th drink.

Roses are red
Lilies are white
I love you, Billy,
Morning, noon and night.

Roses are red
Violets are blue
Your sisters are pretty
What happened to you?

WHEN YOU . . .
THE WEDDING FORMULA

The autograph book verse that begins with the formulaic, "When you get married . . ." may be the most popular of all forms collected in the St. Louis area. Interestingly, the verse always relates to marriage that will CERTAINLY happen. There has never been an autograph verse collected starting, "IF you get married . . ." This is recognition of the lore of girls who were most likely to write in these books. But it is also a warning and a commentary on what their perceptions of marriage were, how the theme of the ball-and-chain marriage has pervaded the autograph book genre, how having children is inevitable and sometimes troublesome, and, in many cases, how the wife needs to assert herself. These were early feminist sentiments, often expressed, long before the headlines declared them. Notice, too, how marriage connotes separation from friends, sending them to a farm, across the river, or up a hill.

When you get married
And your husband gets cross
Pick up a broom
And show him who's boss. (1939)

When you get married
And live by a jail
Put up a sign
Kids for sale. (1943)

When you get married
And have 25
Don't call them a family
Call them a tribe. (1950)

When you get married
And live in a tree
Send me a coconut
By C.O.D. (1952)

When you get married
And live by the lake
Send me a piece
Of your wedding cake.

When you get married
And work on the farm
Send me a letter
As long as your arm. (1933)
     (Working on a farm was exile and a punishment for marriage?)

When you get married
And your husband gets cross
Stamp your foot
And say, I'm the boss! (1934)

When you get married
Don't marry a flirt
But marry a man
That you can make eat dirt. (1931)

When you get married
And live across the river
I'll kill my cat
And send you its liver. (1951)

When you get married
And live in a shanty
Please tell your children
To call me their Aunty.

When you get married
And live in a home
Teach your children
To leave me alone. (1957)

When you get married
And have 24
Call it an army
And win the next war. (1946)

When you get married
And live in a truck
Order your children
From Sears Roebuck.

"ADVICE ON LOVE" VERSES

When you and your boyfriend
Are standing at the gate
Remember love is blind
But the neighbors ain't.

When you're washing dishes
And are mad as mad can be
Just squeeze the old dishrag
And think you're squeezing me.

Twins are bad
Triplets are worse
Sleep by yourself
And play safety first.

Beware of boys with eyes of brown
They kiss you once and turn you down
Beware of boys with eyes of black
They kiss you once and never come back
Beware of boys with eyes of blue
They kiss you once and ask for two
You will meet all kinds of boys
So just beware of boys! (1970)

You may fall from a steeple
You may fall from above
But for heaven's sake, Gladys
Don't fall in love. (1942)

Some girls like tulips
That grow in the park
But Gladys likes two-lips
That kiss in the dark.

Gladys with her sweetheart
Their lips were tightly pressed
The old man gave the signal
The bulldog did the rest.

When you meet a man
Who lives by the levee
Be very careful
Don't get in his Chevy!

Susie, Susie, take my advice
Don't be a mother before you're a wife.

Fall from a steamer's burning deck
Fall from a horse and break your neck
Fall from the starry skies above
But never, never fall in love.

PHILOSOPHICAL, SENTIMENTAL, AND RELIGIOUS VERSES

When this life on earth is over
And this road no more we trod
May your name in gold be written
In the autograph of God.

When you grow old and ugly
As some folks do
Remember you have a friend
Who's old and ugly too.

When the golden sun is sinking
And your mind from troubles free
When of others you are thinking
Will you sometimes think of me?

If I ever go to Paradise
And do not see your face
I'll pick up all my valuables
And go to the other place.

Tho' we meet early
Tho' we meet late
I think we will meet
At the dear Golden Gate.

Joy will dance the whole world through
But it must always begin with you.

When you're sitting all alone
Thinking of the past
Remember there is one true friend
Whose love will always last.

Oranges and lemons grow in Florida
Bananas do too
But it takes Missouri to grow
A peach like you.

Leaves may wither
Flowers may die
Friends may forget you,
But never shall I.

Don't worry if your job is small
And your rewards are few
Remember that the mighty oak
Was once a nut like you.

In your chimney of remembrance, count me as a brick.

Love many, trust few.
And always paddle your own canoe.

Reach for the moon
If it be too high
Be content to grasp
A star as it goes by.

When I am old and cannot see
Look at this verse
And think of me.
When I'm in heaven
And feeling blue
Dig a hole
And pull me through.

MISCELLANEOUS VERSES FROM THE CLASS CLOWNS

My father's a butcher
My mother sells the meat
And I'm the little wienie
That runs around the streets.

God made the rivers
God made the lakes
God made you.
We all make mistakes.

I saw you in the ocean
I saw you in the sea
I saw you in the bathtub
Oops! Pardon me!

To the prettiest girl in the world from the biggest liar in the world.

When you get old
And think you're sweet
Take off you shoes
And smell your feet.

Rich girls ride in taxis
Poor girls ride in trains
Mary Lou rides in police cars
And gets there just the same.

When you get older and get out of shape
Remember girdles are $1.98. (1933)

When you get old and out of shape
Remember face transplants
Are only $120,000.98! (2004)

It's all there in the folk texts of autograph book verses: rhyme, the rites of passage, love, advice, maturity, sincerity, religion, the future, advice, commands, pretending, confusion, hope, joking, insults, self-consciousness, but most of all tradition. For the writer and the receiver there is a need to leave a past and to have a past. And that personal history remains no matter how complex or confusing the world becomes.

Even those who don't remember such verses find a need to leave their legacy. Consider this:

When it rains, it rains
When it snows, it snows.
(I couldn't think of anything else to write) (1932)

CHAPTER 3

THE RHYMES OF KIDS
FROM "FUDGE, FUDGE" TO "EENIE, MEENIE, MINIE MOO ST. LOO"

RHYMES OF COUNTING, JUMP ROPE, GAMES, PARODIES, OR EVEN INSULTS ARE undoubtedly the most remembered folk texts from childhood. Adults of all ages can recite the rhyme required to play a game or choose sides or jump a rope. It is a remembered lore, again learned in an informal setting, but ingrained in the society for generations using the same theme rife with variants.

Real-world concerns, although not fully understood at the time, were raised or parodied in the rhymes kids recited in a sing-song fashion. But these issues were—and still are—the manner in which kids try to understand the world of the adult.

First of all, knowing rhymes for all occasions solidifies a kid's position in a play group. She could be a leader with all the folk rhyming at her fingertips. And then there are issues of courtship, or democracy at work in choosing sides, or marrying, childbirth, even relationships with siblings, parents, or teachers. Often, too, folk rhyming allows the kid in all of us to say things that are not permissible in "polite" society but are tolerated in the charming effect of the childhood rhyme.

COUNTING-OUT RHYMES

Who will be chosen to be on the side of the leader? Or who will be chosen to be "IT?" How will that person be chosen? Does majority rule? Does the biggest kid make the selection? Are there any rules stated? Do kids learn the rules in a formal setting in school and apply them on the streets? What if a kid is chosen last, or worse, not chosen?

Is he a pariah? Does he not know the folk rules? Are there ways to alter selection methods?

All these questions are within the concerns of the child at play. But each of them has an application to the world of the adult that the child will confront and join soon enough. In what ways will he be chosen in the "real" world of his profession? How will she succeed? Who has the control? How can you circumvent the system?

Children may not recognize these applications to their future adult state, but they are the matter of basic teamwork or cultural tradition necessary to learn to "get ahead." And just as in the ritual of American adulthood, the apparent randomness of the counting out realistically decides who is chosen in an absolute manner, or so it is supposed. Children learn to use counting rhymes to suit their patterns. If they want to stagger the rhythm of the verse to make sure their finger points to a desirable target, they do! If they want to speak very quickly or very slowly to ensure the "best" team, they do! Counters can decide the outcome of the counting in their own way.

But also reflective of adulthood, when they are challenged for their "mis-counting" rhymes, they can be called on it. Kids' democracy then can get ugly!

Perhaps the most famous of all the counting-out rhymes is the following:

Eenie, meenie, minie, mo
Catch a tiger by the toe
If he hollers, make him pay.
Fifty dollars every day.
My mother told me to pick this very best one.
Y-O-U spells you and you are NOT it.

Several adult elements are in this rhyme. Complain to the "boss" and you are fined or punished in some way. There is control in life and it must be recognized. This also reflects the capitalist society and

spending. The verse has changed over the years because the fine was at one time five dollars, then twenty, then fifty, then one hundred, and lately the verse is sung with $1 million being the figure. Are the changes in meanings obvious? Becoming a millionaire is an ultimate goal more and more attainable in America.

Also, the authority figure of the mother is always in this verse. A folk saying tells us, "Mother Knows Best," so the jumper, using her own cadence to match her choice, picks the "best" one. But the kicker comes in the surprise at the very end, where the one pointed to is not chosen. Just the opposite occurs; he/she is not picked to be on the team. Instant jubilation is quickly turned into sadness and bitterness. The real world?

More than any other rhyme, this counting-out rhyme has changed more to reflect the society in the use of a specific word as the object of the "catching." "Tiger" is the most popular word used today as a "safe" word. But "n****r" was the most popular word in the rhyme in St. Louis of the 1940s and 1950s. And it even made a comeback in the 1990s, again, sadly, reflecting the times.

Versions of the rhyme have used the following words instead of "tiger:" terrorist, Iraqi, Polack, Dago, German, Krauthead, Queer, Lesbian, Aggie, Newfie, Dutchman, Hoosier, Bag Lady, Russian, Honky, Bosnian, and even The Mayor! It's not difficult to place these folk terms in the historical perspective of St. Louis. Aggie, it is assumed, refers to people from Texas; Newfie is a name for a Newfoundland resident, with connotations of being stupid. Bosnians are immigrating to St. Louis in large numbers. Dutchman is a term for a St. Louis south sider. Honky is a slur word for a white person. Dago is slur for Italians. Hoosier has many connotations in St. Louis, among them, "white trash" and "hillbilly." The other words have their own applications.

So counting-out rhymes are kids' fun? Simple and charming? Could be, but the awareness of adult life is certainly apparent!

POPULAR COUNTING-OUT RHYMES FROM CHILDHOOD IN ST. LOUIS

Aka, baka, soda cracker.
Aka, baka, boo.
If you mother chews tobacco
OUT go you!
> (Sometimes sister is used instead of mother. Both are considered "abnormal," so you should be out of the game.)

Dog S**t you're it! OUT!
Phil the Gorilla S**t, you're it! OUT!
> (Phil the Gorilla was the star attraction at the famous Saint Louis Zoo. Phil's stuffed body was on display for years, and it was later replaced with a statue.)

Monkey, monkey, bottle of pop
On which monkey do we stop?
One, two, three
OUT goes he!

Monkey, monkey, bottle of beer
How many monkeys are there here?
1, 2, 3, mother caught a flea
The flea died and mother cried
O-U-T spells OUT!

Monkey, monkey, bottle of pee,
How many monkeys do you see?
1, 2, 3, my mother took the bottle of pee
The monkey died and mommy cried.
O-U-T spells OUT!

My mama and your mama were hanging out clothes
My mother punched your mother right in the nose.
What color of blood came out of her nose?
(Names a color)
B-L-U-E and you will be the ONE!

This became a St. Louis favorite in later years:

My mom and your mom were dancing naked in space
My mom punched your mom right in the face.
What color of blood came out of her cheeks?
G-R-E-E-N and you will not be IT!

And this is yet another variant:

My old lady and your old lady were sippin' the juice
My old lady hit your old lady and knocked her teeth loose.
What color of blood was mixed with the juice?
R-E-D and you will be the ONE!

Eenie, Meenie, Catch a Weenie
Ali Baba Boo
Coochie, Coochie, Coochie, Coo
I don't choose the big fat YOU!

Another very popular form of choosing teams or making someone "IT" was the "potato" rhyme. Sometimes when the circle was formed, each participant was called a "spud." And when both hands were put in the circle, they also were spuds. The counter in the middle—the one with the most power—would sing.

One Potato, Two Potato, Three Potato, Four
Five Potato, Six Potato, Seven Potato, More!

At the word "more" the leader would hit the fist of one of the "spuds" who would then put that hand behind his back. And the count would continue just until the one person had both hands behind his back. He would then be "IT."

However, if someone did not like the way the person was being chosen because of the cadence of the caller or appearance of favoritism, he could call "kings" and the game would stop. If he had his fingers crossed when he called "kings" the counting would stop. If he did not, he was out of the counting-out process altogether. Sometimes, the majority would call "no kings," and the counting progressed. In some areas of the city the word "bags" was used to stop the counting and the leader could say "no bags." Again, the appointing of the "IT" kept going.

Also, when the counting was not going well for one participant, he could call "times" to tie his shoe or pull up his socks or whatever, and then the game would begin again.

Too many "kings," "bags," or "times" spoken by one person who was having a bad-luck day being chosen was not looked upon very kindly by the rest of the gang, and the decision to "punish" the offender by kicking him out of the process was immediate.

Again, with children, the "politics" of play allowed for rules to be broken, the majority to speak, and perhaps not the best person chosen to be "IT." In the adult world of work some of the same rules apply.

Some later St. Louis versions that speak to the "sophistication" of the child are also popular to count out:

Piss, s**t, baby-poo
Dog poop and turtle dung
OUT go you.

One, two, three, four
Take your ass out the door.

Red, white, and blue
Your father is a Jew
Your mother is a Chinaman
And so are you.
One, two, three, four, five
Take a dive.

Prejudices still exist; mature themes are more popular; slur words are still used. The person is still chosen "IT," but the counting rhyme reflects a different language and theme.

JUMP-ROPE RHYMES

The jump-rope rhyme is the most popular combination of playing games and using meter to further the action. Two kids—who often don't have your best interests at heart—turn a rope while you are skipping to a rhythm. You are singing a rhyme to avoid tripping on the rope as the beat is paced, but the turners can increase the pace or even attempt to "smoke" you. This makes it even more difficult to jump, but it helps your popularity if you can jump without missing and at the same time are familiar with many rhymes.

Sometimes the rhymes command action like turning around, touching the ground, or even calling someone else into the jump as you leave without getting tangled up in the rope. All this takes dexterity and coordination that are difficult for some to master. What follow are competition and jealousy and the strong desire for "Mary Jane" to miss!

Jumping rope in the schoolyard or on the sidewalk is almost exclusively the domain of the young girl. Boys were playing rougher games like "Murder Ball" and "Smear the Queer!" But the coordination of the young girls, which develops earlier than boys, allows her to show her "stuff" and be the "queen of the yard."

And just as in other folk rhymes, jump-rope verses speak to adult themes like marriage, babies, courtship, even violence and taboo topics like abortion. As in other lore, the themes reflect the culture and change to meet the needs of the group, but follow a traditional rhythm. The act of jumping itself can be a reflection of adult life. The "turner" is not as "pretty" as Mary Jane. And, of course, Mary Jane, the prettiest of the girls, attractive to all the boys, knows the most verses, rarely misses, and never has to turn the rope! Jealousy convinces the "turner" to "smoke" the rope in a "pepper" rhyme, which causes Mary Jane to miss! Then she has to turn the rope! What joy! What foreshadowing of the adult world! What a learning experience!

Again, all the verses were learned away from the formal setting of the classroom, but they reflect and represent the real concerns of the folk group of young girls. Some themes are obvious, others need reflection. Consider some samples:

> Cinderella dressed in yellow
> Went upstairs to kiss her fellow
> How many kisses did he give her?
> One, two, three, four, etc.

> Cinderella, dressed in yellow
> Went upstairs to kiss a fellow
> Made a mistake and kissed a snake
> How many doctors did it take?
> One, two, three, four, etc.

> Cinderella, dressed in yellow
> Went downtown to see her fellow
> On the way her girdle busted
> How many men were disgusted?
> One, two, three, four, etc. (1945)
>   (The reference to girdle makes this an older rhyme, of course.)

There are many examples of the "Cinderella" verse. But all use the same fairy tale princess in the verse. Of course, she married the prince and lived happily ever after! But the reference to kissing her boyfriend is a mature theme and the "snake" has various other connotations not usually discussable in public or even completely understood by the young girl singing the verse.

Down in the valley where the green grass grows
There sat Carol all alone.
Along came Don.
How many kisses did he give her?
One, two, three, four, etc.

Down in the valley where the green grass grows
There sits Donny sweet as a rose
Along came Janet and kissed him on the cheek
How many kisses did he get?
One, two, three, four, etc.

Down in the valley where the green grass grows
There sat Janet sweet as a rose
She sang, she sang, she sang so sweet
Along came Johnny and swept her off her feet
How many kisses did he give her?
One, two, three, four, etc.

Again, there are many variants of this rhyme. Note that in one she is lonely, in the other she is the "actor," and in the last one she is "acted upon." The jumper, at the number of kisses she chooses, stops the rope between her legs. Again, this is an indication of her jumping prowess and her understanding of "love."

Even children know that women have the babies. They are not so sure of the method, but their themes skirt the issue and reveal some of their confusions:

Fudge, Fudge, call the judge
Mama's got a newborn baby
It's not a boy, it's not a girl
It's just a baby.
Wrap it up in toilet paper
Throw it down the elevator
How many floors does it fall?
One two, three, four, etc.

Some interpretations of this verse, which was very popular in the 1940s and 1950s, believe it's sibling rivalry at work. The rope jumper has a new brother or sister. She is no longer the only child to get all the attention. So she suggests what to do with the baby.

Other interpretations speak to the "horror" of the verse as it applies to current themes. The reflection is pure folk. The term "fudge" is sometimes used as a euphemism for stool; children would not understand the real term. And the bodily function that produces the "fudge" comes from the same area from which the baby is delivered—from "mommy's tummy." And a judge must be called in because a crime was committed by the mother. The jumper doesn't even recognize the sex of the child—doesn't even care; it's just a baby—just wrap it up in "toilet paper!" Connections to "fudge" are apparent. The child is waste and must be flushed, but not down a toilet—throw the kid down the elevator shaft. It will surely not return and the jumper will be the only child again.

This is sibling rivalry taken to another level. But considering that lore helps explain the world to ourselves, it gives us a reason why things occur, and makes sense of things that are not understandable! Is there merit in this theory?

In the past decade, the rhyme has had a resurgence of popularity. The subject of abortion is also spoken of more often and what all that means is certainly not understood by children. They hear that a baby dies, and to help them understand the concept the jump-rope verse expresses their feelings. Earlier verses of the same rhyme wrapped the baby in "tissue paper" as if it were a gift. The change to "toilet paper" shows the way in which folklore truly reflects the culture.

How veiled are the references in the following popular rhymes of jumping rope?

Miniminihaha went to see her papa
Papa died. Minimini cried.
Mini had a baby. His name was Tiny Tim.
She put him in the bathtub to teach him how to swim.
He drank up all the water. He ate up all the soap.
He tried to eat the bathtub but it wouldn't go down his throat.
Mini called the doctor, Mini called the nurse.
Mini called the lady with the alligator purse.
In came the doctor, in came the nurse.
In came the lady with the alligator purse.
Out went the doctor, out went the nurse.
Out went the lady with the alligator purse.
And now Tiny Tim is home sick in bed
With soap in his throat and bubbles in his head.

I met my boyfriend at a candy store
He bought me ice cream
He bought me cake.
He brought me home with a bellyache.
Mommy, mommy, I feel sick
Call the doctor
Quick, quick, quick
Doctor, Doctor, will I die?
Count to 100 and you'll be alive
1, 2, 3, 4, 5, etc., I'm alive!

Old man Daisy
Set the table
Don't forget the salt
And PEPPER.

> (At the word "pepper" the
> turner spins the rope very
> fast to test the skills of the
> jumper.)

Lady, Lady, please tell me
Who my husband is going to be
Rich man, poor man, beggar man, thief
Doctor, lawyer, merchant, chief
Butcher, baker, candlestick maker
Tinker, tailor, cowboy, sailor
Lady, Lady, please tell me
What my dress is going to be
Silk, satin, calico, rags
Lady, Lady please tell me
What my ring is going to be
Diamond, ruby, sapphire, glass.

Policeman, Policeman
Do your duty
Here comes Susie
The bathing beauty
She can wiggle
She can waddle
She can do the kick
And I bet you all the money
She can do the split.
    (At the action words, the jumper performs the motion indicated.)

Teddy bear, teddy bear
Turn around
Teddy bear, teddy bear
Touch the ground
Teddy bear, teddy bear
Go upstairs
Teddy bear, teddy bear
Say your prayers
Teddy bear, teddy bear
Turn out the light
Teddy bear, teddy bear
Say good night.
    (Again, at the word for actions, the jumper performs the appropriate
moves.)

Little Sally Ann, crying in a pan
Weepin' and cryin' for a nice young man
Rise, Sally, rise, wipe your cryin' eyes
Put your hands on your hips
Let your backbone slip
And shake it to the east
And shake it to the west
And shake it to the one
Who you love best.

Shake it little momma
Shake it all you can
So all the boys around you
Can see your underwear
Rumble to the bottom, rumble to the top
And turn around and turn around
Until you make a stop. (1996)

Not last night but the night before
Two little robbers came knocking at my door
I went up to let them in
And this is what they said.
Little girl, little girl, turn around
Little girl, little girl, touch the ground
Little girl, little girl, throw us a kiss
Little girl, little girl, get out before you miss.

The adept jumper performs all the actions without missing and even adds flair as she moves, e.g., touching the ground with two hands or turning around twice in one jump.

Recent jump-rope versions of this rhyme have used "Mexicans" instead of robbers. Is this a reflection of the current debate over immigration?

Ladies and gentlemen, children, too
This little lady's going to boogie for you
She's going to turn around
She's going to touch the ground.
She's going to shimmy, shimmy, shimmy til her drawers fall down
She never went to college
She never went to school
But when she came back, she was a nasty, nasty fool. (2005)

It's easy to find reflections of the society in folklore. The folk express themselves in ways which are not formal, and often unconscious, but meaningful. Taken by themselves the jump-rope rhymes are full of meaning for the American culture. Combined with the actual jumping itself, performance lore takes on a different slant. A folk game is involved on one level, but on another there is a clue to the definition of the American.

ST. LOUIS INSULTS, RETORTS, TAUNTS, JEERS: ALL BASES ARE COVERED!

Teasing is as much a part of the maturation process of the child as the actual physical growth. Taken to the extreme it may constitute bullying, but in its normal progression, when a child insults a peer, or responds in rhyme as in a retort, this can be evidence of power. The object of the insult tries to counter the jeer and, if successful, is viewed as capable in the eyes of his peer. Often, too, insults can create an emotional response that can lead to more teasing and more rhyming, and then a verbal sparring takes place. The competition can produce leadership qualities in some kids that are admired by their pals. If the folk game being played leads to frequent rule changes, for example, arguing through rhyme can be powerful.

Sometimes, the real world of sexual "differences" is used in retort rhymes to note that some part of the anatomy not usually mentioned, or perhaps not fully understood by the caller of the rhyme, can be permissible in the folk text. Here, power—the power of knowledge—is displayed by the "mature" kid.

Even adults are the objects of insults and retorts. They are authority figures, and they are sacred in their role in the culture, especially if parents or teachers. Kids can, on their own terms and away from the adults, show how "grown-up" they are by taunting, which becomes more serious when one's mother or father is "dissed." It takes great power for the person doing the insulting or retorting, and usually the respect of his peers follows.

Insults or retorts also prepare the child for the real-world embarrassment that is bound to occur on occasion in his adult life. If he can parry the verbal insults of his peers as a kid he will be better prepared for life as an adult.

All these folk types are, again, part of living in the folklore of the child. And the measure of his response is a direct measure of his maturation. Learning how to argue, respond, or negotiate as a child can produce more success as an adult.

What time is it? Two hairs past a freckle, half past a monkey's ass.

Make like a banana and split.

Make like a drum and beat it.

I'm rubber and you're glue. Everything you say bounces off me and
    sticks to you.

I see London, I see France
I see Susie's underpants.
They're not purple; they're not pink.
But boy, oh boy, they sure do stink.

Made you look
You dirty crook
You stole your momma's food stamp book (or pocketbook).
Turn it in, turn it out
Now you know what welfare's all about.

John, John made a big poot.
The engine train went toot toot
And everyone there went kapoot!

Johnny's mad, and I'm glad
And I know what will please him
A bottle of ink to make him stink
And a little girl to squeeze him.

The one who dealt it smelt it (response to flatulence.)

Close your barn door before the horses get out.
(to a boy whose fly is open)

Do you have a license to sell hot dogs?
(to a boy whose fly is open)

It's snowing down south of the "gravois."
(to a girl whose slip is showing)

Mama mia
Papa pia
Little Jennie's got diarrhea.

Janie's a nut
She's got a rubber butt
And every time she wiggles it
She goes putt putt.

Hi ho, Hi ho
It's off to school we go
With razor blades and hand grenades
And BB guns to shoot the nuns
Hi ho, hi ho. (1993)
(This one is more recent. Note the use of weapons in the rhyme.)

Your ass is grass and my fist is a lawn mower.

Let's play horse. I'll be the front end, you be yourself.

You're so ugly when you were born your mother called you a treasure
    and your father said, "Yeah, let's bury it."

The only difference between your mother and Phil the Gorilla is five
    pounds.

I don't shut up
I grow up.
But when I see you
I throw up.

Twinkle twinkle little star, what you say is what you are.

Be like the Blues. Get the puck out of here.

Your mother drives a beer truck.

Give me no lip, potato chip.

Green, green you aren't very clean.

Your mother wears army boots.

I'm going to cut you so low you'll need an umbrella so that the ants
    won't piss on you.

I'm going to cut you so low you'll have to look up to tie your
    shoelaces.

In response to name calling:

A queer is a drip
A drip is a drop
A drop is water
Water's nature
Nature's beautiful
Thank you for the compliment.

There seems to be no limit to the variety of insults, retorts, taunts,
and jeers that kids use. In the St. Louis region, they reflect the same
meanings as in other parts of the country. Kids learn by "standing up
for themselves" through a verbal dodge ball. The differences come
from regional references. But all of them can serve a purpose: prestige,

embarrassment, put-downs, cooperation, negotiations, competition, sexual awareness, or simply disturbing the status quo. All kids, and even adults, seem to know how to use them.

HAND CLAPPING RHYMES: MISS MARY MACK LIVES ON!

Hand clapping rhymes, almost exclusively the domain of young girls, are still very popular in schoolyards, at pajama parties, or just with two friends in the lazy days of summer. More than any other folk type, these rhymes foster friendship and a bonding between the girls who perform them, from as few as two to as many as twelve. There is a cadence required for each to maintain; a pattern of clapping hands on the proper beat; recognition of real expertise when the rhyme is performed successfully and faster each time it is attempted. The bond of the lore fits the folk group exactly and cannot be duplicated in any other venue. In later years, women often execute the same clapping rhymes in a nostalgic performance without missing a beat. The informal learning of the rhymes created the lasting memory and the undying bond.

The themes, also, reflect the concerns of the young clapper. She may be in a circle with a bunch of friends or in an intimate game with one other person, but her thoughts are of the real world and the events of adulthood. It is repetition for a purpose and underscores the importance of having friends united by a commonality. Some observers even opine that girls are socialized through clapping games because the repeated patterns, the "proper" way to sing a verse and clap at the right time, the need to maintain the "correct" verse, and even the absence of the opposite sex, prepare the young girl for adulthood. Then she must "repetitively" do the dishes, make the bed, clean the house, clean the toilets, shop for groceries, change the diapers—over and over and over as is her "fate" in life. The folklore reflection of the ultimate goal of marriage is connoted in this interpretation. Feminist perspectives do not endorse the analysis, but it cannot be denied that hand clapping rhymes are still very popular today by girls of any age.

I'm a pretty little Dutch girl
As pretty as can be
And all the boys in all the world
Are chasing after me.
My boyfriend's name is Dewey
He comes from old St. Looie
With a pickle on his nose and twenty-eight toes.
That's the way my story goes.
    (Some continue with the following verse. Notice again the appearance of the
    snake!)

One day while I was walking
I heard my boyfriend call
And this is what I said
I love you very dearly . . .
I love you most sincerely
So I jumped in the lake
To swallow a snake
And came out with a bellyache.

The cutest boy I ever saw
Was sipping cider through a straw
I asked him if he'd teach me how
To sip some cider through a straw
He said of course he'd teach me how
To sip some cider through a straw
So cheek to cheek and jaw to jaw
We sipped some cider through a straw
That's how I got my mother-in-law
And twenty-nine kids now call me "Maw."

This clapping rhyme has changed very little. It is still collected today even though the use of "cider" is foreign to some girls. Some have never tasted cider or even know what it is, but the verse continues with the same words in a traditional way. It's the picture developed by the words that appeals to the bonding. Marriage is the outcome of the boy-girl encounter, and the symbolism of the straw is obvious. Some verses have "sodie" instead of cider, but they are rare. A few I have collected even used the word "Falstaff" instead of cider. This was a St. Louis beer and using it suggested, also, a taboo forbidden to young girls and boys. But the drinking was mature and thus dangerous for young kids performing clapping rhymes. The result was even more adult and dangerous!

> Miss Mary Mack, Mack, Mack
> All dressed in black, black, black
> With silver buttons, buttons, buttons
> All down her back, back, back.
> She went upstairs to make her bed
> She made a mistake and bumped her head.
> She went downstairs to wash the dishes
> She made a mistake and washed her wishes.
> She went outside to hang her clothes
> She made a mistake and hung her nose.
> She could not read, read, read.
> She could not write, write, write
> But she could smoke, smoke, smoke
> Her father's pipe, pipe, pipe.
> She asked her mommy for fifty cents, cents, cents
> To see the boys, boys, boys
> Pull down their pants, pants, pants.

For those skeptics who doubt the cultural reflection of folklore, note Mary Mack's activities: beds, dishes, clothes—and in each of them "she made a mistake."

And she could not read or write, but she could smoke and give money to boys to pull down their pants!

One verse even has the line:

> She went upstairs to make her bed
> She hit her head and now she's dead.

Doing housework becomes deadly in later verses and hand-clapping rhymes. The thinking of the hand-clapper changes with the times. It's a perfect use of a folk text.

And, importantly, this hand-clapping rhyme is still very popular and common in schoolyards around the St. Louis area. The emphasis has returned to the rhythm, cadence, and balance of the clapping itself, but the words are still there and significant.

In the St. Louis of the 1940s, the most popular ending was:

She asked her mother for fifteen cents, cents, cents
To see the elephant, elephant, elephant
Jump over the fence, fence, fence.
They jumped so high, high, high
They reached the sky, sky, sky
And never came back back, back
Til the Fourth of July, July, July.

From elephants to smoking to seeing boys drop their drawers—clapping rhymes have taken on new subjects using the same patterns. But recent clapping rhymes have become more specific, leaving little to symbolism. The following was collected many times in many places:

See see see my playmate
I can't go out to play
Because of yesterday, day, day
Three boys came my way, way, way
They gave me fifty dollars
To lay across the bench
They said it wouldn't hurt, hurt, hurt
They stuck it up my skirt, skirt, skirt
My mother was surprised
To see my belly rise, rise, rise
My father was disgusted
My sister jumped for joy, joy, joy
My brother raised some s**t, s**t, s**t
Because he had to baby sit, sit, sit.

There is a microcosm of the "real adult world" in this folk rhyme; the connections are obvious.

RHYME PARODIES: ON TOP OF SPAGHETTI REVISITED

By the time kids reach middle school or junior high school they have been exposed to many forces affecting their maturation. The media have bombarded them with hype. Parents have tried some moral objectives. Teachers have done their best to instill discipline in learning. But the kid still needs to flaunt his independence and awareness in ways that are permissible in his world. And poking fun at traditions of some earlier times is one way to declare independence: the parody of the nursery rhyme, the domain of babies; the parody of the patriotic song, the domain of an adult; the parody of advertising, the domain of the work world; the parody of authority, the domain of those "over 18." Playful in their parody, serious in their purposes, these verses allow the child to enter the adult world by making his own decisions while staying in his own milieu.

> On top of Old Smoky, all covered with blood
> I shot my poor teacher with a forty-five slug.
> I went to her funeral, I went to her grave.
> Some people threw roses; I threw a grenade
> The grenade went boom; and that was the end
> Of my poor teacher who was not my friend.

> Row, row, row your boat
> Gently down the stream
> Throw your teacher overboard
> And listen to her scream.

McDonald's is your kind of place
They serve you rattlesnakes,
Hot dogs up your nose
French fries between your toes,
And don't forget those chocolate shakes,
They're from polluted eggs.
McDonald's is your kind of place.
The last time I was there,
They stole my underwear,
I really didn't care,
They were a dirty pair.
They next time you go there,
They'll serve my underwear.

This parody was popular in the 1970s in St. Louis and has made a comeback recently, probably attributable to the discussions surrounding fast food diets. Again, it represents kids' attempts to get involved, but without the power.

Mine eyes have seen the glory of the burning of the school
We have tortured every teacher and have broken every rule
We have hung Sister Mary on the flagpole of the school
As the brats go marching on.

Glory, glory, hallelujah, Sister hit me with a ruler
I hit her on the bean with a rotten tangerine
As the brats go marching on.

More recent verses include the following:

Glory, glory, hallelujah, teacher hit me with a ruler
So I met her in the attic with a semi-automatic
Now she ain't my teacher any more.

Pepsi-Cola hits the spot
Ties your belly in a knot
Tastes like vinegar, looks like ink
Pepsi-Cola is a stinky drink.

Hail Mary, full of grace
Bless my boyfriend's happy face
May his hands that are so strong
Make them stay where they belong.

Now I lay me down to sleep;
My car is parked across the street
If it should roll before I wake,
I pray the Lord put on the brake.

Oh say can you see
Any bedbugs on me
If you do, pick a few
'Cause I got them from you.

Beginning in junior high and continuing through college, nursery rhyme parodies are very popular. Sometimes called "Goosed Mother Rhymes," they represent the ideal attempt of the young person to declare adulthood and abandon childhood. Leave the rhymes to the babies, they seem to imply; my own rules and world view, however they shatter the sacred, are more important to me.

Mary had a little lamb
Boy was the doctor surprised.

Mary had a little lamb
Her father shot it dead
Now it goes to school with her
Between two hunks of bread.

Jack and Jill went up the hill
To have a little fun
Jill forgot to take the pill
And now they have a son.

There was a little girl who had a little curl
Right in the middle of her forehead
When she was good, she was very, very good
But when she was bad . . .
She got a fur coat, jewels, a condo, and a sports car.

Little Miss Muffet
Sat on a tuffet
Eating her curds and whey
Along came a spider
And sat down beside her
And said, "What's in the bowl, b***h?"

Hickory, dickory dock
The mouse ran up the clock.
The clock struck one
And the other escaped with minor injuries.

They start out with Patty Cake as babies, continue through clapping rhymes and jump-rope rhymes with adult themes, and then conclude with deliberate flaunting of the kids' world—folk rhymes come full circle. But they always reflect the society that tells them and repeats them in the traditional pattern. They have been used that way for decades in St. Louis and other regions; and they will only get more creative and reflective as the maturation of the child occurs at an increasingly earlier age.

CHAPTER 4

RIDDLES AND JOKES
HOW CAN YOU TELL IF YOU'RE FROM ST. LOUIS?

ARGUABLY, THE MOST POPULAR RIDDLE IN AMERICAN FOLKLORE IS THE conundrum, a joke based on the use of a pun in the question or the answer. What is black and white and read (red) all over? Using the oral tradition where the words are not read, but spoken, which is a critical part of the definition of folklore, the answer would be more obvious. But when asked of a person, the conundrum, with a pun in the question or answer, has different answers, and this also is a criterion of folklore.

If you answer a "newspaper" to the question, you were probably born before the 1940s or spent your youth in the 1940s and 1950s. The joke was very popular in those decades and even before. But if you answered: an embarrassed zebra, a skunk with diaper rash, a bleeding penguin, a wounded nun, or even Fidel Penguin, you could have been born in any decade from the 1970s through the 1990s. The question reflects the culture that asks it, with answers also reflective of the period.

Most answers are silly, not plausible, but oblique enough for the teller to suggest a rebellion to the common answer and sophistication and cleverness that smack of superiority. The "wounded nun" answer was collected from a Catholic nun! It appeared in the jokelore after Vatican II in the mid-1960s. Presumably, such jokes could not be told in public before the effects of Vatican II, but after Vatican II so many dogmatic traditions relaxed and joking on such topics became acceptable. The function of folklore connoting openness or saying what is not permissible in a permissible way operates here.

51

If you answered "Fidel Penguin," your play on the word "red" adds yet another dimension. Fidel Castro is a communist by ideology, and the popular colloquialism for the doctrinal beliefs is RED. But in an absurd and "groaning" joke, Fidel is a penguin, black and white, and a correct answer to the question.

All answers to the question are correct. They all indeed are black and white and read/red. So the joke serves its purpose: the joker caught the listener in a pun, perhaps showed his superiority to the inferiority of the listener, maybe taught the listener a thinking process, perhaps introduced "punning" as a literary device, and could have, very importantly, bonded in a way he never could have done with plain conversation.

Riddles and jokes all perform a service. Depending on the culture, the interaction, or the age group, the effect can be different. But since the legend of the Sphinx, riddles have been part of man's oral tradition and used in literature, mythology, and folklore. It is the latter where contemporary jokesters live their folk traditions most.

Consider Halloween, for example. Trick or treat usually involves a joke by the costumed witch in order to get a treat from the adult at the door. If the adult answers the joke question, there is that possibility that the Halloween visitor won't get the treat. But often the joke cycle is such that the same joke is told over and over the same night. This is an annual repetition. So the adult has to pretend he does not know the answer. Then the child has some knowledge the adult doesn't have, and as a bonus the kid gets the candy. (By the way, this tradition of trick or treat seems to be connected to St. Louis. Theories abound as to why it exists in the St. Louis region almost exclusively. Some point to the number of Irish who settled here since the origins of Halloween are mostly associated with Ireland.)

This function of a learning experience, in some form, is the basis for many jokes or riddles. Also, the superiority/inferiority function applies in the question/answer format. The riddler always feels a sense of superiority, usually unstated, in knowing the answer that the listener doesn't know. If the listener happens to know the answer, the "educator riddler" can be demoralized or made to look inferior, if not stupid.

Jokes, too, can be used by "sophisticated" kids who have outgrown the "silliness" of the simple joke and start telling "sick" jokes, "sick" puns, or "gross" jokes. This attempt to shock is also a function of joking and permits what is not permissible. Perhaps there is an underlying current of joking about a serious illness or a gross bodily function that connotes that this is not happening to me and to joke about it is one way of understanding the disease or illness. It cannot be explained away, the thinking goes, so let's joke about it, hoping to keep it off a personal level. Even adults love to tell these sick jokes as part of a bonding ritual. Adults, getting older daily, become more and more aware of the things that can happen to their bodies as they approach old age. Joking can relieve the anxiety.

Riddles, too, can be used directly as education. There is a logical process in the question and the answer, and what seems contradictory or implausible actually is not. So creative thinking is encouraged in some quarters through riddles and jokes. In the competitive American society, contests, often unstated, develop, and a sense of "great intelligence" is experienced if someone answers the riddle correctly. Here, again, superiority is a function. Consider the oral transmission of the joke: How many animals of each kind did Moses take on the Ark? The answer, of course, is that Noah had the Ark, not Moses. But when the riddle is put into the oral tradition, it is, by testing, answered more than 90 percent of the time as TWO. The riddler catches the person with an answer that should be very obvious except that the respondent was not listening carefully. Or take these examples: Do they have a Fourth of July in England? Can a man living in North Carolina be buried west of the Mississippi in St. Louis? If a rooster lays an egg on a roof top, does it slide to the left or to the right? Do you pronounce the capital of Florida as My-ami or Mee-ami? The answers are more obvious in written form but the oral transmission of folklore makes them more traditional. Each, however, is designed to stump the listener and make him feel inferior. Even though it is "only" a joke, studies have shown that people associate high IQs with answering these types of questions correctly. But there is no correlation. Again, the importance of joking in American society is evident in this judgment.

Another aspect of the superiority function is the riddle question in response to what is perceived as a stupid query. Instead of calling the person who asks an obvious question ignorant, the joker simply responds with an obvious answer. Is the Pope Catholic? This is the most popular version of this form of folklore. Ask whether today is Sunday, for example, and if it clearly is, then the Pope question is the response. Unstated is the sarcastic comment: Don't ask such obvious questions.

St. Louis folklore has many examples of these joke/riddle forms of folklore. They are not all endemic to the region because the transmission of jokes can be all over the world in seconds. But there are some versions that are very popular in the area and reflect some aspect of the culture of St. Louis in their variants. Is the Gateway Arch in St. Louis?

YOU KNOW YOU'RE FROM . . . TOASTED RAVIOLI AND BUDWEISER?

A relatively new folk genre with jokelore is the formulaic expression that ascribes funny, sarcastic, or ironic statements of specifics to a peculiar region. And the "in" joke is immediately recognizable to the native of the area, thus making the riddler and the listener closer members of the "in" crowd, who "get" the reference, can laugh about it, and feel a sense of bonding with the knowledge.

The Internet has made this genre quickly acceptable and appropriate to many cities of the world. The anonymity of the origins is directly related to the tradition of folklore, and the traditional formula used makes it even more folk specific.

The St. Louis metropolitan area is easily identified in this joke format:

YOU KNOW YOU'RE FROM ST. LOUIS WHEN . . .

- Vacation is a choice between Lake of the Ozarks and Silver Dollar City.
- You love toasted ravioli with Budweiser beer.
- L.A. is not Los Angeles but Lower Affton.
- Velveeta is your favorite cheese.
- You have fond memories of the Highlands.
- You display your nun-whipped knuckles with pride.
- You call "Grand Leader" your favorite department store.
- You've "done it" on Art Hill and lived to tell about the experience.
- You wore green to school on Thursdays.
- Teen Town was the highlight of your week.
- You know that the Pink Sisters are not a rock band.
- "Sliders" are your favorite munchies after midnight.
- You believe you can get anywhere in twenty minutes.
- You know what a pork steak is and what barbeque sauce to put on it.
- You think the four major food groups are Imo's, Budweiser, Ted Drewes, and pork steaks.
- You've said, "It's not the heat; it's the humidity."
- You still can't believe the Arena is gone.
- Your first question to a stranger is: "Where did you go to high school?"
- Your wedding reception has "muskacholli," ham, roast beef, and green beans.
- You can find Pestalozzi Street by the aroma.
- You still believe that Mavrakos made the best chocolates.
- You believe that Whistle is a gourmet soda.
- You think of the Twin Cities as Festus and Crystal City.
- You know that Falstaff was not a Shakespearean character.
- You know that 905 is not a time to meet someone.
- You believe that cream soda should always be red.
- A getaway weekend is a trip to Alton.

- A Hoosier lives south of Chouteau and not in Indiana.

- You think that no furniture store can compare to Slacks.

- Your malt can be turned upside down and not move.

- You know WHY people go to the "east" side.

- You are a member of the River des Peres Yacht Club.

ST. LOUIS RIDDLE POTPOURRI: CONUNDRUMS TO CATCHES TO SILLINESS

Why do they send Bud to school?
To get Bud-weiser.

What's the difference between a St. Louis woman and River des Peres?
River des Peres is a busy ditch.

Why did the St. Louis kid take his ladder to school?
He heard it was high school.

What's the common thing among the Veiled Prophet, the Blues' Stanley Cup, and a smart Ladue woman?
They're all make believe.

What do St. Louis women make for dinner?
Reservations.

What did the Pasta House salad say to the refrigerator?
Close the door, I'm dressing.

What's the difference between a St. Louis mother and a vulture?
A vulture waits until you're dead to eat your heart out.

What's the difference between a VP socialite and a vulture?
Nail Polish.

What's barbeque in Imperial?
A fire in a garbage can.

What is luggage in Arnold?
Two shopping bags from Wal-Mart.

Why can't St. Louisans swim in the Mississippi?
> *They'd leave a ring.*

Who has an IQ of 300?
> *Barnhart.*

What is the biggest decision of a Southsider before he goes to a dance?
> *Whether to wear red or green socks.*

What's a "10" in St. Louis?
> *A "5" with money.*

What's perfect sex in Kirkwood?
> *Simultaneous headaches.*

How can you tell there's an elephant in your freezer?
> *Footprints in the Ted Drewes.*

What's a seven-course meal in Dutchtown?
> *A hot dog and a six pack.*

What's the difference between government bonds and St. Louis men?
> *Bonds mature.*

Why did the St. Louis kid take his ladder to Busch Stadium?
> *He heard the Cards were playing the Giants.*

Why did the Ladue golfer bring two pair of pants to the golf course?
> *He was afraid he'd get a hole in one.*

How do they take a census on Cherokee Street?
> *Roll a quarter down the street.*

These are only a few of the jokes or riddle forms that are specific to St. Louis. All the formulaic joke forms such as Knock-Knock, Elephant, Polack, Mary Jane, Moron, Sick, Dead Baby, Helen Keller, Dolly Parton, even Hamburger Jokes were, and are still, popular throughout the St. Louis region. Indeed, folklore has made them specific to the area by using one of the formulas and inserting a reference specific to the St. Louis region.

By transmitting a recognizable joke formula with obvious references, both the joker and the listener understand the bonding inherent in the allusion. They are more likely to develop further lore related to the same region. A useful stereotype sometimes results and a migratory lore is created.

Developing a St. Louis variant of a formula joke may make it permissible to say something not acceptable in polite conversation but often acceptable in the form of a joke. Some observers even believe that jokes of a regional area, which on the surface appear to be negative, add diversity awareness to a region that is critical in the full development of the potential.

Value can be added, it is argued, by an understanding of the thought process behind the allusion. Consider the following.

SEVEN REASONS WHY ST. LOUIS IS QUIET ON SUNDAYS

(Insert the any of the following: Jews, Italians, Irish, African-Americans, Bosnians, Hispanics, Polish)

1. The _____ are visiting relatives in Ladue.

2. The _____ are all putting flowers on graves.

3. The _____ are sleeping off hangovers.

4. The _____ are all in jail.

5. The _____ can't get their cars started.

6. The _____ are in custody in the local immigration office.

7. The _____ think it's Tuesday.

Whatever your reaction to the list, every group mentioned has served as an informant for the joke tale. They get it! And the humor involved becomes a starting point, for them, for discussions on diversity. Perhaps an important lesson in understanding, valuing, and tolerance will result. No joke is ever told in a vacuum.

CHAPTER 5

MOMISMS
MOM AND CLEAN UNDERWEAR—
ACCIDENTS HAPPEN!

MORE THAN ANY OTHER CHAPTER IN THE FIRST *PASSING IT ON*, THIS ONE
on Momisms elicited the most responses. Everyone could recall things
their mother said, and they often thought their mother was the only
one using the "momism" as her lore! An even more frequent comment,
however, was, "O My God, or OMG, I've become my mother!"
Informants told me that they "swore" they would never say the same
things their mother did. At the time, they seemed so meaningless and
filled with empty threats. Others wondered about their "dad" comments
as they had a hard time even remembering them! So the introduction is
still operative as a good definition of the American character. The new
pronouncements of Mom may spark more memories of your youth!
Have you become your mother?

Ever since Alexis de Tocqueville tried to define what it means to
be an American in his seminal work, *Democracy in America*, published in
1835, countless others have attempted the same definition. Some say
generosity, others mobility, some the "melting pot," some even that
violence best defines *the* quality that characterizes Americans.

Prominent among American Character research studies also is the
notion that Mom, or the American Woman, best defines the way in
which Americans organize their culture. The conclusions revolve around
manners, morals, etiquette, traditions, and even guilt—all the domain,
they believe, of the American Woman. And it is in these areas, according
to the research, where the continuity of a culture resides.

If Mom is indeed the definition of the American, folklore can add some supporting evidence in the abundance of folk expressions attributed to her. They are transmitted orally, informally learned, traditionally expressed, and used by every generation of "mother" throughout American history.

St. Louis mothers have used the following expressions for years. As an inheritance they were passed on and continue to be circulated even today. As the Baby Boomers look in the mirror they really do see their mothers.

MOMISMS

- Never use the toilet during a thunderstorm.
- Always put toilet paper on the seat of a public toilet. You could get a venereal disease.
- Don't ever lean back at the movies; you'll get ringworm.
- If you leave, don't come back!
- Good. Leave. I'll pack your lunch and your bags!
- I don't care if Jesus Christ himself is singing, turn it off and come to supper NOW!
- Be careful what you wish for; you might get it.
- Always give some money to a poor person. He may be Jesus in disguise testing you.
- A lady never uses a toothpick.
- There are plenty of other fish in the sea.
- You pays your money and you takes your chances!
- If you don't wash your hands after going to the bathroom, the germs will go to your brain!
- You have an answer for everything, don't you?
- Don't come into the kitchen unless you're bleeding or unless your arm is hanging by a thread.
- Never drink out of a water fountain. You never know who's been

there before you.

- As long as you live under my roof, you'll do as I say.
- You don't have to like me, sister; I'm your mother!
- So what if it's raining? You're not sugar; you won't melt.
- Never be in bed during a thunderstorm.
- Don't cross your eyes or they'll stay that way.
- It will never heal if you keep picking it.
- Always wear clean underwear; you never know when you might be in an accident.
- I don't care if you like them or not; you're related.
- Don't worry. It's only baby fat.
- The world is your cow, but you've got to do the milking.
- Wash behind your ears or potatoes will grow there.
- If you want to be beautiful you have to suffer.
- A lady never sits with her legs parted.
- When you live with a goat, you'd better get used to the smell.
- Only slutty girls wear half slips.
- When you invite a young man to dinner, don't use a white tablecloth; it will remind him of bed sheets.
- You know you don't have to marry every boy you go out with.
- A good wife always has lemons in her refrigerator.
- Always make your bed in case the house burns down.
- It's just as easy to fall in love with a rich man as a poor one.
- Why should a farmer buy a cow when he can get the milk for free?
- Don't play with matches; you'll wet the bed.
- What will the neighbors say when they see that get-up?
- As long as your feet are under my table, you'll do as I say.
- One more time and I'll smack you into tomorrow.
- You bought what? You ain't got two nickels to rub together!

- Remember: Always keep one foot on the floor at all times.

- You'll thank me when I'm dead and gone.

- You'd make Elizabeth Taylor join a convent. (or Madonna or Paris Hilton, etc.)

- Never wear white after Labor Day.

- Don't wear your best underwear to the doctor's office. They'll raise the price of the visit.

- Never sleep on the bedspread. It's a sure sign of laziness.

- Ladies don't sweat; they glow.

- Never drink wine out of a plastic glass.

- I didn't buy all those clothes for you just to decorate your closet.

- Girls who pierce their ears get what they deserve!

- Were you born in a stable? Close the door!

- You sleep in an unmade bed? You were not raised that way!

- Eat those Brussels sprouts. Think of all the starving children in China.

- Remember: twenty-seven chews to a bite.

- Never drink tea except out of a china teacup.

- Never go swimming right after eating. Wait at least an hour.

- Save yourself for your husband.

- He's OK, but what does his father do?

- Nothing worthwhile happens after midnight.

- Young lady, I'm not asking you, I'm telling you.

- The sun doesn't rise and set around you, you know!

- Don't talk back to your mother.

- If you go to bed with wet hair, you'll turn gray before you're forty!

- This is not a hotel!

- A woman can never have enough Tupperware.

- I never wanted kids. I did it because your father wanted them.

- If you ever strike your parents your hand will stick out of your grave.

- You'll eat it and you'll like it!

- Always remember: panties up, dress down.

- Remember what food you don't clean up from your plate now, you'll have to eat all of it before you die and are allowed into heaven.

- Never pick your nose; your head will cave in if you do.

- Are you lying? Stick out your tongue! It will always tell me!

- A little birdy told me.

- Remember: When you get older, beer is for whores.

- It's never lady-like to drink from a bottle.

- OK, sister, don't get me started!

- If you fall, I'll kill you!

- Always eat pretzels completely through before you swallow.

- The best gift to your future husband is your virginity.

- OK, I understand, but how long does this "gay" thing last?

- If you knew your homework as well as the *TV Guide*, you'd get "As" in everything!

- I hope you have a child just like you someday.

- I could out-stubborn anyone until I had you.

- The food's hot? Sorry, I haven't learned to cook *cold* yet!

- Look, girly, this is not a debate!

- If you do something bad, I'd better hear it from your mouth first, not someone else's.

- Remember: Every "double" is bad: double chin, double belly, double donuts, double trouble, double chocolate!

- You'd better enjoy going to the movies with grandma or do you want her to stop paying your tuition?

- Fair? That's where you take your pig for a blue ribbon! Don't talk to be about fair!

- Always keep your knees together and your hands folded in your lap.

- You have two options for dinner: Take it or leave it.

- You ought to start your own church.

- Don't let your mouth write a check.

- If you fall and break your legs, don't come running to me.

- Don't you dare look at me in that tone of voice!

- Do you kids realize how lucky you are?

- If I want any s**t from you, I'll squeeze your head.

- If you're fat, you'll never get a boyfriend.

- Eat what you can and then finish the rest.

- Tell me who did it, and I promise I won't be angry.

- Remember: God doesn't give with both hands.

- Move just one pace from the corner and I'll slap you into tomorrow.

- If you want breakfast in bed, you should sleep in the kitchen.

- Fine with me. Wish in one hand and s**t in the other. See what fills up first.

- You know, sister, I brought you into this world and I can take you out of it.

- Do you really want me to give you something to cry about?

- I think you'd argue with a signpost!

- Do you want a knuckle sandwich?

- Oh, yeah? I haven't smacked anyone on a Wednesday in a loooooong time!

- If God wanted a hole in your tongue He would have put it there!

- I'll smack you so hard your brother will feel it.

- Are your hands broken? Pick it up yourself; I'm not your maid.

- Do you live only to annoy me?

- Never try on anyone else's glasses or you'll go blind.

- Stick out your tongue and it'll stay that way.

- I do not know where your shoes are; it's not my day to watch them.

- Ass. Bed. NOW.

- Can't died in the poor house. (When you respond to something: "I can't.")

- Do you want to spend the rest of the day picking your teeth off the floor?

- Eat chocolate in the morning and you'll get worms.

- You want to end up like those people?

- If you have bigger friends it will make you look thinner.

- I'm not yelling; I'm helping you hear.

- You know, you can always walk out whenever you want.

- I never used to get angry before I had you kids.

- OK, sister, either eat it or wear it!

- If you're going to kill each other, do it outside. I just finished cleaning.

- Start praying. If it does not come out of the carpet, you're dead.

- Tell lies and you'll get bumps on your tongue.
- Just go to your room and think about what you did.
- Any nutjob within 100 miles would find you!
- I would have never talked to MY mother like that.
- Go put on a sweater, I'm cold.
- Don't worry, you have to eat a peck of dirt before you die. A little won't hurt.
- I'm going to give you to the count of three and then it's over for you!
- When did your last slave die?
- You know, you're too much like your father.
- You know you are getting on my last nerve.
- What? You just ate an hour ago?
- If you learn something from me, it's worth it!
- Hear me now and believe me later.
- Finally, father's advice: If momma ain't happy, ain't nobody happy!

Often, these expressions are so deep in the subconscious that after they are expressed, they surprise. When did I last hear that? Why am I using it these many years later? Will my kids remember them? The answer is in the folklore.

CHAPTER 6

SUPERSTITIONS

RUB YOUR "BILLIKEN"

THE MASCOT OF THE SAINT LOUIS UNIVERSITY ATHLETIC TEAMS IS A Billiken. Origins of the mascot are pure folklore and exist in different versions. Apparently, a Missouri art teacher, Florence Pretz, designed the image of the Billiken for the Billiken Company of Chicago in 1909. The image became a piggy bank, dolls, and other collectibles by about 1911. By 1912, the Billiken images had lost their popularity. But the coach of the SLU football team, John Bender, had been aware of the Billiken in 1911 through his acquaintance with some sportswriters. As the legend goes, Billy Gunn—say that ten times quickly and hear the name—owned a drugstore near the university. He was close to the athletes and the coach. Gunn recognized Coach Bender with the greeting, "You're a real Billiken." Sportswriters overheard the conversation and the name stuck as a mascot. Other stories attribute the name to different sportswriters at different events, but all of them involved Coach Bender. Soon Bender's Billikens were all over the city. And the rest, as they say, is history.

Among national scholars of popular cultures who specialize in the subject of sports research, the Billiken was recently voted the quintessential collegiate mascot! He was already an icon when chosen for the SLU teams, but his status has grown over the decades. To the whole world the Saint Louis U. teams are known simply as "the Billikens."

Not surprisingly, there is a large statue of this Buddha-like figure in the middle of the SLU campus. It serves as a daily reminder of the spirit of the institution. But it is open to touching, caressing, rubbing, and wishing, and not just by athletes. Legends abound about the contagious magic of this icon: pass a test, finish the thesis or dissertation on time, do well in the oral examination, be admitted to a curriculum in SLU graduate school or be admitted to SLU, get a date for the homecoming, beat Dayton or Xavier—all it takes is a bow to the smiling, rotund figure you pass every day.

Of course, the Billiken is represented in all manner of collectible items. Buying a likeness means good luck, but it is better luck to have one given to you. And the best luck of all is to have the Billiken stolen and then returned to you!

So the athletic symbol has become the "campus" symbol for everyone. The rubbing or touching the body of this icon transmits positive thoughts, and a fully developed belief is created. Folklorists call this a superstition! But call somebody "superstitious" and one might as well call someone a pagan, because the connotation of the word speaks to an age of wizardry, ignorance, uneducated fluff, and the domain of the lowest classes in a society. And yet the Billiken is touched hundreds of times a day with the reasoning, "Well, it can't hurt!"—but not the admission "I am superstitious."

The pattern of denying any superstitious belief seems very common in the St. Louis area. There has been no scientific, folkloristic study to compare St. Louis with other cities or regions, but of the 100,000 items collected for this research, 30,000 are superstitions—is "folk beliefs" a better term?—from the informants in the St. Louis region. Loudly and uniformly they protest their devotion to any "silly ritualistic pattern," but not one informant has denied throwing a bouquet at her wedding, or being "attacked" by rice, or currently bird seed, as she leaves the church, avoiding black cats or ladders, and most often, remembering 13 on a Friday!

The etymology of the word "superstition" comes from the Latin *superstitio*, meaning "standing in terror of the deity." Since the beginning of oral history there has always been an allegiance to the "gods," who were hovering around us during every activity, either ordaining or condemning our actions. We knock on wood today for good luck, or at least to acknowledge those "spirits" around us who might "control" our future just as the Druid priests of ancient England knocked on trees before they undertook a task. But we don't know or care about the origins of the "knocking," we just do it as it has been done, ritualistically, for centuries. We recognize that we are in control of what we are about to do, but it can't hurt to have some "divine" help along the way!

But we, especially St. Louisans, continue to deny that we are superstitious. Call a folk belief what you will—old wives' tale, folk belief, customary habit, family ritual—it is still grounded in some recognition of those "forces around us."

Most superstitions in the St. Louis area, as in other regions, classically revolve around the "rites of passage." In birth, marriage, death—the tipping points of the cycle of life—because of their significance of entering a new phase of life, we seek the positive, the best outcome, the most optimistic result. We all want the help of those "unseen deities" to make sure that each step in the maturation process is positive and, we hope, perhaps even abundant.

Within each of those hallmark periods of passage, however, is life itself. And the beliefs in St. Louis—whether folk cures, weather predictions, children's learning, courtship rituals, dating habits, daily activities—or a host of other experiences—are purely folklore and have been traditionally transmitted in this historic region.

Importantly, also in St. Louis there is a form of belief that relates to a conversion. If a mirror is broken, for example, it means seven years of bad luck. This is a widely known belief. However, in St. Louis it is believed that if the pieces of that broken mirror are thrown into running water, as in a stream or a river, the bad luck is negated or neutralized. The interpretation of this and other conversion phenomena can perhaps be understood in a few different ways. People in St. Louis do believe in superstitions and are aware of the consequences. Perhaps the American character trait of optimism is reflected strongly in this belief and others, and St. Louisans believe in the power of the optimistic attitude. Maybe the "traditional St. Louisan" needs to pay homage to the "gods" of the mirror, for water is a cleansing and makes thing new.

Whatever the reflection of conversion superstitions, they are present as a definite pattern in St. Louis beliefs. Not every folk text has a conversion, but those that do are clearly remembered and practiced by many in the region.

Following are some of the superstitions collected. They are meant to be representative, familiar, and most common in St. Louis, but certainly not exhaustive.

BIRTH, INFANCY, CHILDHOOD

Never cut a baby's fingernails before he's one year old. Otherwise he will grow up to be a criminal. One must always "bite" them off—the maternal practice of "nibbling." (Several informants even believed that a child's hair must not be cut before one year, fearing the same result, and even nibbled the hair!)

Conversion: It's OK to cut the baby's nails before one year as long as the clippings fall into an open Bible. This will void the back luck of growing up to be a thief.

Also, as a conversion, if the hair is cut before the child is a year old and kept in a safe, secret place by the mother, the child and family will grow prosperous and live to a very old age.

If a woman is scared by something during her pregnancy, the baby will have a birthmark in the shape of that which scared her.

This is a very popular folk belief in St. Louis. Dozens of stories were collected about the objects that scare pregnant women. And pictures were produced to "prove" the belief! Misshapen rabbits, snakes, deer, birds, skunks, and even ghosts (!) have been blamed for causing the indelible "mark" on the infant. Of course, the mother "remembers" the time it happened, even though she may not have known about the folk belief when it did.

For example, St. Louis native Patty Bausch recalls:

Around 1912, Grandma Nellie Keller, as my mother tells me, had a baby she named Vivian. The baby was born with a streak of grey hair. Grandma believed that if something was wrong with a baby, it was caused by something that had happened during the pregnancy and the baby was "marked" by it. While pregnant with Vivian, Grandma had called a neighbor she had a disagreement with "an old grey-haired man." Mom said she may have actually used a stronger noun! Sadly, the baby lived maybe a year or so; however, I don't think her death was contributed to the grey hair. But Grandma Keller did.

Birth is a rite of passage, and all parents pray for a healthy, "intact" child. The fear of something being "wrong" with the baby is always there. So if a mark, however slight, may appear on a newborn, something or someone, not the parents, must be blamed. In all important aspects, the child is perfect, but that one blemish—even if not seen by anyone—had to have a reason for existing. And the reason is not usually accepted as medical.

The first pair of a child's shoes should be hung around the mirror of the car for good luck.

To predict the sex of a child "for certain," the man must remove his wedding ring, and with the woman lying on the floor and him standing above her, ties a piece of string to his ring. He holds it very close to the woman's stomach, but not touching her, and remains very still; the ring he is holding will move either in a circle or a line. A circle means that the baby is a girl; if a line, it's a boy!

Never give a child fresh fruit during its second summer. It will get very ill with diarrhea and could dehydrate.

Never bring a newborn to someone's house before you bring it to church. Bad luck will follow.

Family luck will be better and more prosperous if the first child is a boy. "I wish you first a baby boy, and when his hair begins to curl, I wish you then, a baby girl," as the verse goes.

If a woman craves a certain food during her pregnancy, she must be given that food as soon as possible. If she is denied the food, the baby will be born with a birthmark shaped like the food.

Never show a baby its image in a mirror before he is a year old. He will be cursed with bad luck all his life.

Babies born in the summertime are more intelligent than those born at other times of the year.

Never teach a little girl to whistle; she will become very hairy.

If a baby is born with a veil or caul, he will be very bright and also be able to predict things. (A caul is an intact amniotic sac over the face.)

Put a child's tooth under a pillow to attract the "gods" who will replace it with money. Our "god" is called the Tooth Fairy! (Ancients believed that baby teeth saved and put into the coffin when the person dies will complete the cycle of life for him or her and make his or her judgment positive.)

When coming home "for the first time" a child must be carried *up* the steps before he is carried *down* any steps to ensure good fortune in life.

Rub a child's gums with whiskey when he is teething.

Blow smoke in a child's ear to cure an earache.

Born on a Friday is bad luck unless it's Good Friday and then it's good luck. Some people report "holding on" until Saturday for the birth of their child!

If a child is born during a blue moon, he will be rich the rest of his life.

A woman loses two teeth for every child born to her.

Always place objects in a baby's right hand. If he grows up to be left handed, he will be shunned the rest of his life!

Place a bell or some other noisemaker in or on the baby's crib to scare away the evil spirits.

If a child is born with a tooth, he will grow up to be a murderer.

LOVE, COURTSHIP, MARRIAGE

The superstitions surrounding marriage almost exclusively relate to the behavior of the woman. There are things she *must* do on the wedding day; things she has to do before she gets to that day; and even in courtship, she is encouraged to practice mating rituals such as picking daisy petals to discover her true love.

All these beliefs, so pervasively applied to women, underscore the ideal of marriage in society and the Cinderella-like dreams with which women are culturally acclimated.

Men follow mating customs in folklore that are not superstitions, *per se*, but practices that guide the boy-man along the path of the hunter. Is he having the right experiences in dating? Does he know the correct "lines" to use? Does he do the asking for a date? Is he seen with the "proper" girl? Is he sexually experienced? Does he know how to exaggerate if he is not?

These folk customs are learned informally. There is no formal education the man must undergo, but following courtship rituals correctly is important to his cultural standing. So it is the woman who maintains the folk traditions of love and marriage, for the most part. And except for the man throwing the bride's garter—acquired, by the way, in a "manly fashion"—the woman is responsible, according to lore, for the success of the marriage.

If a woman is a bridesmaid three times she will never get married. **Conversion:** She can convert this "bad" luck by becoming a bridesmaid seven times and then she will be married.

Catching the bouquet at a wedding reception guarantees marriage for the receiver within the year. However, if the woman who catches the bouquet was married before, this brings bad luck to the bride as a "magic of transference."

Never remove the wedding ring, because doing so will break the marriage.

A stye can be removed by rubbing it with a wedding ring three times.

The bride must wear something old, something new, something borrowed, and something blue on her wedding day. But the old must be given to her by a woman married for more than fifty years. The new item should be a handkerchief because a woman always carries one wherever she goes. Something borrowed must come from someone in the wedding party, most often the maid of honor. And something blue should come from a favorite, respected relative, because the color blue represents truth and candor, which every marriage must have.

A bride must wear a penny in her shoe on her wedding day. The penny must have been put in her shoe by the man who walks her down the aisle. Anyone else doing it will cause bad luck.

Place a piece of wedding cake under your pillow and if you dream of the same person three nights in a row, you will marry him/her.

A blessing for every raindrop that falls on your wedding day.

Sisters must never get married in the same year. One will surely be divorced.

A bride must be carried over the threshold of her first home so that the spirits in the wood don't harm her.

A bride must cry at the first kiss from her new husband or her life will be full of tears.

Choose the right month in which to marry:

Married in January's hoar and rhyme,
Widowed you'll be before your prime.
Married in February's sleepy weather,
Life you'll tread in time together.
Married when March winds shrill and roar,
Your home will be on a distant shore.
Married beneath April's changeful skies,
A checkered path before you lies.
Married when bees over May blossoms flit,
Strangers around your board will sit.
Married in the month of roses, June,
Life will be one long honeymoon.
Married in July with flowers ablaze,
Bittersweet memories in after days.
Married in August's heat and drowse,
Lover and friend in your chosen spouse.
Married in September's golden glow,
Smooth and serene your life will go.
Married when leaves in October thin,
Toil and hardship for you begin.
Married in veils of November mist,
Fortune your wedding ring has kissed.
Married in December's cheer,
Love's star shines brighter from year to year.

So it's good to be married in June, August, September, November, and December. But one must avoid January and October. If you want money, choose November. If you want to avoid relatives, don't marry in May. And July will cause you to consider some "if only's." Married in April will be OK, but never predictable.

Consider your name change when you marry: Change the name and not the letter, change for the worse and not the better.

It is bad luck for the groom to see the bride's wedding dress before the day of the wedding. Only bad luck can follow.

The top layer of the wedding cake must be made in the favorite flavor of the groom and then frozen until the first anniversary, when it is shared by the couple. The groom is not supposed to know the flavor so that he will have good luck in the "second" eating of the wedding cake. If his bride, by chance, had the wrong flavor of cake made, it means that the marriage will not last.

Throwing birdseed, not rice, at a newly married couple as they leave the ceremony is for fertility and monogamy. Birds, according to folklore, choose their mates for life and remain monogamous. It is hoped that the birdseed will create a magic of transference to the happy couple.

DEATH AND FUNERAL FOLK BELIEFS

If a bird flies into your home, someone will die within a year. This may be the most popular superstition in St. Louis! It was collected dozens of times and told "as true" by many informants who immediately related with their story of the deceased relative. During one of my call-in radio programs at KMOX (CBS) in St. Louis, with the legendary Jack Buck as host, one caller related the bird belief in his life, but for him it had to be a black bird. Mr. Buck, with his facile mind and impishness, remembered a similar personal story.

It seems that his grandmother in Ohio believed the superstition about the bird, and when her husband, Jack's grandfather, died, she blamed the bird. She remembered telling everyone about the superstition when she found the bird. And on her husband's death, she repeated her warning. The only catch, as Buck recalled, was that his grandfather died some ten years after the bird appeared in the house! Something has to be blamed for the rite of passage of death, no matter how long it took.

There is a conversion to this superstition: After the bird is removed from the house, one must go through each room and sprinkle holy water everywhere to ward off the evil spirits. In this way, the bad luck will be voided.

If a person dies in the house, the mirrors should be covered so that death doesn't take any more people who live in the house.

If a picture falls from the wall for no apparent reason or a broom hits the ground when no one is near it, you will hear of a death of a close friend or relative very soon.

A pregnant woman should never visit a funeral home because the spirit of Death might inhabit the child.

Never count the number of vehicles in a funeral procession because yours will be the next funeral.

If you meet a funeral procession on your way to a vacation, turn around and go home.

If you meet a funeral procession crossing in front of you, you will not reach your destination.

Conversion: Remove your hat as respect to the "gods of death" and you will have nullified the bad luck. Or, if you are not wearing a hat, make a small, polite bow to the deceased in recognition that it is the destiny of every man. This, too, will negate the bad luck.

If one dreams of a marriage he will hear of a death.

Funeral cakes, the favorite recipe of the deceased, must always be eaten on the day of burial to ensure a happy eternity for the individual. (Again, the magic of transference is applied here to remember the happy times. The cake is made and eaten as an antidote to the sadness of death.)

A dog howling during the day is a sign of impending death of someone near.

A person will die an easier death if his head is to the east when he dies or is dying.

In many St. Louis families, it is very common at yearly reunions or even at family get-togethers to believe that if everyone shows up some-one at the reunion will die within the year. There is always relief uttered when someone can't make it at the last minute or if someone fails to show up. That means that the family life will go on; it is actually good luck not to have the whole crowd together.

Open all the doors and windows in the room where the deceased actually died so that the spirit of death can leave quickly.

The clocks in the house of the deceased must all be stopped until the departed is buried. When this is done, there will be "no more time" for death to strike anyone else.

When telling someone goodbye as they leave in their car, never watch the car until it is out of your sight. If you do, someone in that car will die.

MISCELLANEOUS SUPERSTITIONS: GET THAT HAT OFF THE BED!

For good luck always hold your feet up in the car when driving over railroad tracks.

Never throw away the egg shells until after the cake is baked. Otherwise it will not be delicious and it may cause illness to those who eat it.

You will get the first hard frost exactly 6 weeks after you hear the first katydid.

Seating thirteen at a dinner table is bad luck for everyone eating at the table. Jim Dowd III, of Webster Groves, recalls that his aunt was acting "funny" at one Thanksgiving. She did not want to eat at the table and said she preferred to eat in the kitchen. Everyone wondered whether she was ill or if someone had hurt her feelings. It turned out that if she sat down at the table for Thanksgiving she would be the thirteenth person and everyone would have bad luck.

If someone who is invited to dinner fails to show, you must remove the whole place setting or someone who eats at the table will get sick.

If someone opens a pocket knife and someone else closes it, the friendship is cut forever.

If you move to a new or different home, never take your old broom with you. You are bringing all the bad luck from the old home. **Conversion:** You can take the old broom with you if you burn the tips of the broom to rid the bad luck. Fire will destroy it, and you will have a new broom for good luck in your new home.

Always give a new homeowner a freshly made loaf of bread and a carton of salt. The salt will keep the house "seasoned" and the bread will ensure that the homeowners will never go hungry. If the bread is stale it will bring bad luck to the person who gave it because it represents envy.

Never give your true love yellow roses; they symbolize jealousy or guilt.

While you are sweeping the floor, if the broom touches someone's foot, that person will never be married. Similarly, while vacuuming a rug, never ask a person sitting in the way to get up. Ask him/her instead to raise their legs. This will ensure that they will get married. Asking them to get up and leave changes their direction (in life).

Kevin Lakamp, a nurse, reports that nurses often tie the corner of the top sheet in a small knot so the patient doesn't die on their shift. If the patient is critically ill, sometimes a double knot is tied. It is bad luck for nurses to have one of their patients die on their shift.

It is bad luck to rock an empty rocking chair.

Never pass the salt to anyone because it will bring bad luck. The person must always reach for his own salt shaker.

Place a penny in a wallet or purse you give to someone for good luck. **Conversion:** If it's more than one penny, the good luck will turn to bad luck because it would represent greed.

When receiving a live plant from someone, never thank them or it will die.

Always tear the corner of a two-dollar bill so that it will not bring you bad luck.

Kathy Tepe Deachan relates lore from her father, Henry A. Tepe. Mr. Tepe's grandfather was a cobbler, and his parents met at a shoe wholesale shop on North Broadway. After she was widowed for a second time and had two young sons to support, Mary Tepe operated a retail shoe store on Geyer in the front of the family home in Soulard. Five generations with shoemaker roots have learned that you never put a pair of new, unworn shoes on a table. If you do they will never fit you!

This occupational lore is typical of traditional, oral transmission that stays in families for generations, and sometimes it leads to conversion beliefs. There is no explanation for the consequences, but it is very likely that family members will remember and practice the belief forever.

Never fold your napkin after finishing a meal; it will bring bad luck and risk the friendship of the cook.

Never give a knife as a gift without including a coin in the present. One does not want to "cut" the friendship.

To cure baldness, rub the head with extra virgin olive oil and then wrap the head in very warm towels. This belief was told to me during a radio program in St. Louis. The caller swore that it worked, but it had to be "extra virgin" olive oil. The response of the next caller gave another baldness cure: Rub the manure from a black chicken on the head to grow hair! It was the first time that this folk belief was heard, but three callers within the hour relayed the same belief. And research revealed that the practice is popular in Tennessee and Kentucky.

Never allow anyone to pass between you and a companion while walking. This will cause your friendship to break. **Conversion:** If this happens, go back and retrace your steps in order to counteract the bad luck; or say the phrase, "Lucky Strike" and then shake hands with your companion; or say together, "Bread and Butter," and that will void the imminent bad luck.

If a black cat crosses the path you are traveling, it will bring bad luck. **Conversion:** Spit in the direction of the cat, turn around three times, and continue walking in the same direction. This will neutralize the bad luck.

If you have a wart, rub it with your spittle first thing in the morning before you even get out of bed. It will dry up without any medication.

Always sleep with your head to the east to guarantee pleasant dreams.

Never eat the point of a piece of pie first; always save it for your last bite. And when eating it, make a wish. The wish will always come true.

If you find a handkerchief, do not pick it up. Hankies are for tears and touching it will cause you sorrow.

To rid your place of ants, draw a chalk line because ants will not cross chalk.

If you do not cover your mouth when you yawn, the devil will enter your body.

When driving at night past the World's Fair Bird Cage at the Saint Louis Zoo, yell "Finark" to mimic the cry of the birds in the cage. This magic of transference guarantees good luck. The folk vocabulary involved in this belief is pure St. Louis lore.

If you wash your blankets in May, you will wash your loved ones away.

If you tell someone of your plans, they will never come true.

Cutting your fingernails:

Cut them on Monday, cut them for health.
Cut them on Tuesday, cut them for wealth.
Cut them on Wednesday, cut them for news.
Cut them on Thursday, a new pair of shoes.
Cut them on Friday, cut them for sorrow.
Cut them on Saturday, see your love tomorrow.
Cut them on Sunday, the devil will be with you all week.

The larger and blacker the woolly worm, the harsher the winter.

Never place a hat on the bed; it will bring bad luck. **Conversion:** Place three hats on the same bed to void the bad luck.

If you sing before breakfast, you'll cry before supper.

Spilling salt is bad luck that can be converted by throwing some salt over your left shoulder. However, in St. Louis, spilling sea salt or kosher salt is a certainty of bad luck and can never be converted. But sea salt, when used purposely, can ward off evil by placing it in front of the threshold.

When visiting someone unannounced you must leave by the same door you entered. If you do not you will bring bad luck to the owners.

Never plant your spring flowers until the snowball bushes have bloomed. They only bloom in cool weather and the coolness may kill your spring buds.

Mashed potatoes are good as poultices on burns.

Whether it's folk medicine, planting, eating, household activities, or the rites of passage, there are superstitions to cover every aspect. Again, they are informally learned but traditionally practiced and passed on and on and on. They become personal lore that helps us explain the world to ourselves. If we don't like the explanation, we can convert the superstition!

CHAPTER 7

HOLIDAY LORE

DANGEROUS REDHEADS ON NEW YEAR'S DAY TO PICKLES IN CHRISTMAS TREES

IT'S ANY NEW YEAR'S DAY. I WAS OUT LATE THE NIGHT BEFORE. IT WAS cold. Sometimes it was snowing. Seldom was it warm. But there I was standing at the front door of my grandmother's home. It might have been 6 a.m., 8 a.m., or 9 a.m.—never later. I had to be the first person to greet her on January 1 at her home! And I had to do it because I was brown-haired, relatively young, and perhaps superstitious when I didn't even know it.

Here's how this works: The "first footer" is among the most popular holiday folk beliefs in the St. Louis area. A young man with brown hair *must* be the first visitor at your front door on January 1 in order for you to have good luck for the whole year. He is to walk through your home and partake of some of your food in order to have the magic of transference, and then leave from the back door, if there is one. Otherwise he can leave from the same door through which he entered.

Now, if the first person to come to your door is a young man with *red* hair, this is the foreteller of the worst luck. Your whole year will be bad because the red hair is a reminder of Judas, who betrayed Christ. Certainly, he should not be your first visitor. The young brown-haired man represents Jesus Christ, and that is good.

The worst luck, however, would occur if the first visitor is a woman with red hair and a large gap in her teeth. The red hair for the Judas connection combines with the gap teeth for the mark of an evil, wanton woman, just as Chaucer described.

The best luck of all may come to the first footer, however. He is usually paid for his visit, not only with the food he eats but also with money to boot. And there are people in St. Louis who spend their New Year's Day as first footers. They fit the description of the lucky visitor and hire themselves out for the day.

The Slavic culture uses this tradition annually, as do the Scottish. Both claim creation of the practice. Origins may be obscure, as they are for most folklore, but more and more families, not within these two ethnic groups, observe the same ritual almost religiously.

Call it a superstition or a folk belief or an old wives' tale. The label is not important. The practice as identified with a specific holiday is the meaningful application, for January 1 is the beginning of a new year. Time to clean the slate. Time to take stock. Time to introspect. Time to change for the better. Just as the god, Janus, whose name is given to the month, had two faces that looked forward and backward, so do many people on that first day.

If it is the traditional time for resolutions, and if good luck is very often the desired outcome, then why shouldn't people do all they can not to offend the "gods?" So the first footer, connecting Jesus, youth, money, food, and visits, which all connote a rebirth and new life, is as close as the folk can get to a guarantee!

The folklore of holidays is as traditional as the rites of passage and as ritualistic as a prescribed ceremony. Year after year, whether it be Christmas, Easter, New Year's Day, Rosh Hashanah, Valentine's Day, Thanksgiving, or any other holiday, the same folklife is enjoyed and practiced. Without the practices, the holiday would not be the same; the intended outcomes would be in jeopardy; the transmission would not be generational; the day would just be "different." Whether it's the traditional food that is eaten, or the way in which the table is set, or the order of the events, or the way in which a practice is begun or concluded . . . a pattern of lore evolves and helps to bond the group and give them a common purpose.

Holiday lore in St. Louis may not be very different from lore in other regions, but many traditions, such as the first footer, are practiced more fully in this region than in any other. The various neighborhoods and ethnic groups that create the charm of the city's lore have contributed much folklore whose lines of origin are blurred. The value of practicing these diverse holiday customs is in the richness of the transmission. Ethnocentrism takes a back seat to the importance of the holiday ritual.

The folk practices listed for each holiday are representative. Some ethnic groups claim invention, but all of what has been collected in St. Louis is practiced without regard to claiming origin. And the transmission of the lore keeps on and on and on.

NEW YEAR'S DAY

You must eat pork at some time on the first day of the year because the pig roots forward and has direction in life. It will rub off on you as the magic of contagion. If you eat chicken, however, you will have bad luck all year because the chicken roots all over the place for food and has no direction. That will be your fate, too, if you partake of chicken.

Eat herring on New Year's Day or New Year's Eve to ensure a year of wealth. Legend tells us that the "milk" glands in the herring fish correspond to the life, fertility, and abundance in the woman; therefore, it will be good luck and good fortune.

Always sweep the dirt from your house out the front door on New Year's Day so that you are sweeping out the bad luck from the previous year. And if you use a new broom you are guaranteeing good luck.

Eat twelve grapes on New Year's Day, one for each month of the year. After eating each grape, make a wish and the wish will come true. Note: many St. Louisans who practice this belief have frozen grapes at the ready in the event they cannot find them in the grocery stores on the first of January.

Whatever you do on the first day of the year, you will do as a habit in the New Year.

If you sew on the first day of the year, you will be destined to pull out each thread with your nose or teeth as punishment.

Eating cabbage on New Year's Day means that you will never be poor in the New Year.

Shooting off fireworks on New Year's Eve or New Year's Day will scare away all the evil spirits of the past year and help you start afresh in the New Year.

If you make a resolution on New Year's Day it is important to write it down, put it in an envelope, and seal it. Then give it to a friend who will open the envelope in a year to see if you followed your resolution.

Wear some new clothes on New Year's Day to ensure luck throughout the year.

Make certain that none of your cupboards is empty on January 1 because they will stay that way all year and give you bad luck.

Open all the windows in your home at the stroke of midnight on December 31 so that all the bad luck of the past year flies out the window.

Do no laundry on New Year's Day because you will wash away (cause the death of) one of your family members.

Black-eyed peas must be eaten on January 1 to ensure abundance (wealth) during the coming year.

Whoever comes to visit you on New Year's Day must be given some of your food so that good luck will follow you all the year through the magic of transference.

VALENTINE'S DAY

Legends remind us that birds choose their mates on Valentine's Day. Because birds are monogamous, this transference of fidelity will happen to women on February 14 depending on the first bird they see on that day:

- See a blackbird, you'll marry a clergyman.
- See a robin, you'll marry a sailor.
- She a goldfinch, you'll marry a millionaire.

- See a sparrow, you'll live in a bungalow.
- See a crow, you'll be poor the rest of your life.
- See a dove, you will have good luck in any marriage.

Put bay leaves under your pillow on the night before Valentine's Day and you'll dream of the person you are to marry.

Put rosemary in your shoes before you go to bed on February 13. Then wear the shoes all day on Valentine's Day, with the rosemary still in them, and you will be rich when you marry.

Never give yellow roses to your valentine; they signify jealousy. Other colors of roses also have meaning:

- White: Purity
- Pink: Joy and Happiness
- Red: Passion
- Purple: Enchantment
- One Red Rosebud: Purity and Beauty
- One White Rosebud: Girlhood

A woman should give her boyfriend tulips for Valentine's Day because they symbolize virility.

On Valentine's Day, an unmarried woman who wishes to be married someday must cut an apple in half. The number of seeds in the apple will indicate how many children she will have. Children, in the number of seeds, of course, follow the marriage.

A man must awaken his love with a kiss on Valentine's Day to ensure a long relationship.

Giving violets to a lover on Valentine's Day is the ultimate gift because legend tells us that violets were growing outside the jail cell where St. Valentine was kept.

A young lady is to take a dandelion that has gone to seed and blow it. The number of seeds remaining after she does this will indicate the number of children she will have.

Giving a glove to a woman on Valentine's Day is tantamount to an engagement.

Never give chrysanthemums to a lover on Valentine's Day; they are for mothers only.

If you see a squirrel on Valentine's Day you will marry a cheapskate who will hoard money.

EASTER SUNDAY

If it rains on Easter Sunday it will rain for seven consecutive Sundays. Some believe that if it rains on Palm Sunday, it will rain for seven consecutive Sundays.

Always cut your hair on Good Friday; it will grow thick and strong.

It is very good to see a lamb on Easter Sunday because the devil can take the form of every animal except a lamb. For this reason, and because it's not likely that one will see a lamb, it is important to make a cake in the shape of a lamb for every Easter celebration.

One Easter egg must be dyed a bright red color. The person who finds this egg during the hunt will have good luck all the year through.

It is important to wear three brand new clothing items on Easter Sunday as good luck.

It is very good luck to see a robin on Easter Sunday because legend has it that the robin picked the thorns from the crown on Jesus' head and the blood stained the bird's breast.

Holy Thursday is known also as Green Thursday. It is important to eat green things on that day as green symbolizes life and rebirth.

Easter "smacks" are common in some households. Cutting off a new shoot from a plant, and swatting someone with it, especially a child, will ensure that he is protected from disease and will stay healthy, young, and "green." This is a magic of contagion.

If the egg you crack on Easter has two yolks, you will have good luck all the year.

If the wind is from the east on Easter Sunday, there will be good crops for harvest.

Bake a peace cake or "pax" cake for Easter and take it to a person with whom you had a quarrel during the year. The cake is a sign of forgiveness and peace. The cake could be of any flavor.

Egg "nicking" is important to do as a traditional practice. Each person nicks the dyed egg of each person at the dinner table and says, "Christ is risen." Good fortune will follow all the year.

The first Easter egg shelled on Easter Sunday must be divided so that everyone at the table gets a piece for good luck and a holy life throughout the year.

Carol Powell of St. Louis reports that the following practice is Mexican in origin and continues as a tradition for her family:

Egg shells, with the insides blown out, were stuffed with confetti, then colored with markers. On Easter Sunday as a guest arrives or leaves the home, young children are supposed to crack the egg on the heads of adults and wish them a Happy Easter. The confetti represents the colors of spring; the egg, rebirth and youthfulness; and the cracking on the head of adults, the magic of contagion. The Easter dinner table must have a centerpiece of a basket with five colored eggs to represent the wounds of Christ on the Cross.

THANKSGIVING

Pumpkin pie, the most traditional dessert on Thanksgiving, is eaten and served according to a pattern: If the pie is served with the point toward the guest, he will get a letter soon. If the point of the pie is served away (opposite) from the guest, marriage is in the offing within the year. If the pie is served with the point to the left, the guest will get love, if to the right, the guest will get a kiss from a stranger before the day is over.

If a person cuts off the point of the pumpkin pie and eats it first, she will never be married. This relates to girls only.

It is important to cut off the point of the pie and push it to the side of the plate. When the whole piece of the pie is eaten, one must say nothing, eat the point of the pie, drink some water, and make a wish. It will always come true.

Sweet potatoes must never be served on Thanksgiving Day unless they were harvested after the first frost. Otherwise, they will make the people who eat them very sick.

The turkey carcass can predict the coming winter: white, a heavy snow-filled winter; dark or gray, a mild winter.

Put the turkey wishbone over the door of the dining area. The first person to walk under it after Thanksgiving will be married next.

Stewed pumpkin, as a poultice, will relieve swelling.

Make pumpkin seed tea to relieve stomach aches.

To cure warts, rub them with the corn from the Thanksgiving dinner and they will disappear.

Five grains of corn must be placed at each plate as a reminder of the first Thanksgiving when the ration was only five grains of corn the first winter in America. Saving the five grains until the next Thanksgiving will ensure that one does not go hungry during the year.

If it snows before Thanksgiving Day the winter will be mild.

CHRISTMAS

It is believed that the animals talk at midnight on Christmas Eve to welcome the Christ child. Legend tells us that the oxen did not talk that night and even today are forever silent. But the donkey brayed loudly and continues to do so today.

Kissing under the mistletoe, the Golden Bough, hastens marriage plans for many. If the mistletoe is burned on the twelfth day of Christmas, the marriage is guaranteed.

Never wash a Christmas gift of clothing; it will wash out the good luck.

On Christmas Day, place straw around the base of fruit trees to ensure an abundant crop.

The hours of sun on Christmas Day, so many frosts the month of May.

If Christmas is on a Friday, an easy winter will follow. But if Christmas is on a Monday, the winter will be very harsh.

A pickle ornament must be placed in the tree, hidden as well as possible, and the first person to find it on Christmas morning will have good fortune throughout the year. This is a tradition of German origin, practiced by many St. Louisans today. Pickle ornaments can even be purchased to help continue the tradition.

Place four chestnuts on the hearth. Name each one for four men or women you know. The last to burst from the heat will be your husband or wife.

Save the ashes from the Yule log, the log from the Christmas fire, and scatter them on the ground at planting time in the spring to ensure a beautiful display.

Never remove Christmas decorations before the twelfth day of Christmas or you will have bad luck for the year. But if the decorations are left up after the twelfth it will also be bad luck.

Never light Christmas candles until Christmas Day or you will have bad luck.

The Christmas cake, in the shape of a Yule log, should be cut only on Christmas Day and then a slice of it placed under the pillow to be slept on for the twelve days of Christmas to ensure good luck and good fortune.

Break the ribbons on Christmas presents and you break good luck.

Returning a Christmas gift will bring bad luck to the purchaser.

Walking backward around a pear tree on Christmas Day will ensure good luck and good fortune in the coming year.

Never put the statue of the Christ child in the crèche before Christmas Day; it will bring bad luck. And never put the statues of the three Magi in the crèche until after New Year's Day.

The youngest member of the family must put the topper on the tree to ensure a year of good luck.

Holiday lore in St. Louis, as in other regions, covers many aspects of folklife itself. But they are customs, beliefs, or traditions that are celebrated at one time of the year, and one time only. The intended effect of many of them is to ensure an entire year of good luck, good fortune, and even good health. They become holiday rites of passage and are scrupulously observed. Many family traditions often temper the regional practices, making them a special bonding experience for the extended clan and serving as an ideal function of the lore.

Other holidays, not as popular as these represented here, also have their rituals. And their identity and remembrance as in the repeated practice guarantees that the traditions will continue and be tempered by the culture. What happens every Labor Day? Or Fourth of July? Or Halloween? Or Mardi Gras? The lore is there and the transmission is permanent. These holidays are annual opportunities to educate, validate, or compensate within our informal cultures. So next time your doorbell rings on October 31, remember the ritual! And don't break the tradition.

CHAPTER 8

FAMILY LORE
FIND MY DOOHICKEY!

IT MIGHT BE A PRIVATE RITUAL, A QUIET TRADITION, OR THE PRAYER SAID AT bedtime. It might be what happens to baby teeth. It could even be the remembered "crazy" behavior of grandpa. It might be the physical characteristic that shows up on many blood cousins that creates legends. It could be an expression that does not need explanation or a word that has bonded people for decades. It could be baby talk in an adult world. It could even be the imaginary family ghost who becomes a scapegoat for generations. It might be the food that is always eaten on Christmas Eve or the picnic traditions of the Fourth of July.

Maybe your family lore is filled with stories about your favorite pet: When Winky, your parakeet, would wake you every morning with her raunchy vocabulary and the one time she used it in front of your priest guest; when you got your favorite dog who bonded the family; when Mouse was primping in her doggie Christmas collar; when your goldfish went to "fish" heaven via the toilet; when the sensitivity of your animal predicted an event; when your pet passed. These stories will not be forgotten and the future lore may vary with details, but they will all be part of your personal history and no one else's. You will repeat the tales often.

It could be all of these things and more, but it is all defined as family folklore. The genetically bound nuclear group grows with rites of passage, practices the same folklore, and adds new lore from the increasingly extended family, and somehow everyone stays connected in the experience. Within this growing family culture, everyone, especially

93

children, are inspired, educated, strengthened, and filled with hope. Folk traditions can develop the necessary stability from the sense of belonging and the sense of worth. The lore of family enables everyone to understand that there is an invisible bond of love that helps to structure the big events of life. And no matter what educational or intellectual goal is eventually achieved, family folklore remains in the minds of all. Most importantly, it can be passed on to ensure the same stability, acceptance, and love for many generations to come. Family folklore is a concrete reality that does not have to be explained to anyone; it exists ultimately in the hearts of the family members and defines them as nothing else does.

Remember when Uncle Joe did that? Remember that time at the Labor Day picnic? Remember what we used to say when there was not enough food for company? Remember when we could not see the Christmas tree until Christmas Day? Remember those footprints of Blitzen and Vixen under our tree? Remember those socks dad wore with sandals? Remember the bread pudding mom made without a recipe? Remember when we used to sing made-up songs on our way to vacations? Remember the games we played during storms? Remember when Uncle Tom made up funny words to identify people? Remember dad dressing up as a baby on Halloween? Remember when mom could never find her keys (and now I can't)? Remember when we spent vacation at grandma's house? Remember the feather beds? Remember what we each got to do on our birthdays? Remember when they "celebrated" after grandpa's funeral? Remember "steal the present" on Christmas when that rubber chicken showed up for years? Remember dad's malaprops? Remember when Aunt Mary got excited and her heart always "tumped and tumped?" Remember when grandpa couldn't say "cinnamon" or "aluminum" and how they always sounded?

To paraphrase the song, "Try to remember, and when you remember, follow"—your family lore and heart—and you will find yourself. For it is within this strong family lore that we are centered.

FAMILY FOLK VOCABULARY

Words are the basis of any folk text. Within families words define an existence and maintain a life of their own for decades. They are recognized as silly or poor grammar or even "imaginary" words, but they sustain families in an ideal folk manner.

Everyone has a junk drawer. And everyone has a favorite word for something in that drawer known only to the members of the household and foreign to visitors. Get me the "doohickey," or the "thing-a-ma-jig," or the "whatchamacallit," or the "do ma bop," and someone always got the Phillips screwdriver or the hammer or the tweezers. They just knew, as a family, what was needed.

If guests were invited to dinner and something special was being served the family was cautioned, "FHB: Family Hold Back." Every family member heard the command and obeyed, but the guests suspected nothing.

Sometimes for dinner families had "mustgo"—leftovers—everything in the refrigerator must go.

An illness, not perceived as serious, might be "creeping crud," or "fungus-a-mungus," or "toe-shus of the boe shus" or "slithery juice," or "inverted glands."

For some families, who know grammar perfectly well, it "snew" yesterday; he "drownded" in the pool; he was "bornded" in August; we're "undusting" the house; it's raining and "winding"; he "clum" the ladder. All survive through a family's history.

"Grunty" is going to the bathroom.

"Pusghetti" for pasta, "sammich" for sandwich, "front room" for living room, "ice box" for refrigerator, "grip" for suitcase, "pocketbook" for purse, "weskit" for vest—are all folk terms and used for years within family groups.

A popular folk tradition in St. Louis is to scapegoat with a familiar name. Often when something happens in the house—for example, if a picture falls from the wall; if something is momentarily missing; if "no one" ate the last cookie; if the lights were not turned off—it's natural to blame the imaginary member of the family. For some St. Louisans YAHOOTI did it; or the GHOST OF SEVERE is the culprit; even DIZZY DEAN does things secretly; some accuse SATCHEL PAIGE; and sometimes SASQUATCH is the culprit. Whatever the name, the person becomes a member of the family and just as important as anyone else.

"Celery" is often used for "shall we?" "Lettuce" is used for "let us."

Goodbyes are family expressions also, such as the popular, "See you later, alligator." "I'll be like a tree and leaf." "Vamoose caboose." "I'll peel like an orange." "Goodbye, apple pie." "Goin' home to Rome." "Back in a while, crocodile." "Keep in touch; love ya much." Most often the farewell expression is associated with one particular relative whose legend grows yearly as other people recall the saying and even use it with their own family.

FAMILY STORIES AND TRADITIONS

My great-grandfather worked for the Shakers in Kentucky. He was Catholic. On the Holy Day of Obligation on August 15 he wanted to go to Mass in Bowling Green, some fifteen miles away. None of the other Irish were going to go to Mass that far away. So my great-grandfather went to the railroad tracks to see if anyone was going to Mass. No one was. So he got permission to use the handcart but there was no one on the other side of the handle to help him push it. Just then a very nice looking man appeared and asked if great-grandfather wanted some help. The young man said he needed to go to Bowling Green also. They got to Bowling Green, just the two of them on the cart, and great-grandfather left the young man on the tracks while he went to the office to tell them he would return for the handcart. The office people marveled that he had come all those fifteen miles by himself. He told them about the young man who had helped him but they protested that they had watched him pushing the cart all by himself. The family has always felt it was an angel who helped my great-grandfather get to Mass that day.

—Ann Bergman, St. Louis, Missouri

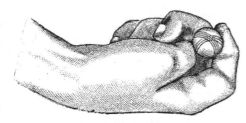

When we were walking on the sidewalk we would say, "Step on a crack, you'll break your mother's back." Naturally, we stepped over all the cracks.

Men and boys played bottle caps in the alley behind the house. They used a broomstick as a bat and the pitcher would pitch the bottle caps, which everyone had saved, to the batter. They made up their own rules before the game started.

In the evening after dark in the summertime, all the neighborhood kids would play "hide and seek." The lamppost on the corner was "home." If you ran and touched it without being caught you were home free.

The boys would play marbles by drawing a circle in the dirt. Each player would put so many marbles in the center. They would take turns shooting at them with a taw, which was the name for everyone's main shooter marble. Whoever ended up with the most marbles got to keep them. Sometimes someone would shout, "Knuckles down," and that boy would have to shoot with all of his knuckles on the ground.

When we wanted one of our friends to come out and play, we would stand in front of their house and shout, "Oh, Lois," because we didn't have a telephone in those days. And even if we did, shouting was the traditional way of asking someone to play.

One of my mother's superstitions was, if you made a mistake and put an article of clothing on inside out, it would be bad luck if you changed it back to the correct side. You had to wear it the same way all day long.

Some of my dad's superstitions were: Never put a hat on a bed. Never put shoes on a table. Never open an umbrella in the house. Never hit anyone with a broom. All of these were supposed to bring bad luck.

One of my husband's superstitions is that when you go into a house or a building by one door, you must leave by the same door or you would have bad luck.

—Juanita Murphy, St. Louis, Missouri

A family tradition for many, many years, is after a delicious meal at Thanksgiving, we would do the dishes together, clean up the kitchen, and get the old candy from years ago and also some new candy—many different varieties of bulk candy—place it all on the table and give each member a 12 x 15 inch piece of plywood, covered with foil. Everyone sits around this huge table and makes his own individual creation of a gingerbread house. We only use eatable materials in this process, by the way. And age is not a factor; everyone is invited to join in. After the decorating is completed, each family member takes their gingerbread house home for Christmas. We find this a great way to keep everyone close to each other. It is an important family custom, even ritual, that we look forward to every year.

—Judy Bisesi, St. Louis, Missouri

Sandra Dannehold, from St. Louis, remembers all the folk beliefs from her family. They were farmers who lived in Waterloo, Illinois, across the river from St. Louis. Their lore is a combination of the family folklife and the ethnicity of the German community. During an interview, Sandra recounted:

I feel as if "they say" should be placed in front of all my folklore. What follows are sayings and beliefs, some would say superstitions, from my whole family. On reflection, some of these folk items were probably picked up from other places, but they were said by my German family members—for all I know, the sayings originated on German farms like ours and spread to the rest of the country.

My parents were born in the twenties and spent their entire lives on farms. Once I started to write these down from memory, I could see how the folklore reflected my parents' life and times. When my parents were young, there was really not even radio—which meant that farmers had absolutely no idea if a storm was on its way or not. One way of dealing with the uncertainty of the weather may have been to look for any signs that might indicate what the weather would be short term. And it would naturally have led farmers to look for patterns in the natural world that might be repeated from one year to the next.

Today, there are many people who know exactly how big a squirrel's ear is. But there was a recent time, at a nearby place, where all this folklore made sense, was relevant, and was totally understood. Come to think of it, they still must have some sense to them because I remember them and have told them to others!

I happily remember all the following examples of folklore of my family:

FOLK MEDICINE

- To cure a wart, take a raw onion or raw potato and rub the wart. Bury the onion or potato without looking at it. By the time it's rotted, the wart will be gone. Important: Don't tell anyone about the cure, and don't look at the wart.

- Wear a string on your ankle for leg pain.

- Carry a small potato in your pocket for arthritis.

- Eat mustard when you have a fever.

FOLK SAYINGS

- He's so crooked he can't sleep in a round house.

- Don't step on the dog's tail while it's sleeping.

- Each sow should sleep in its own slop trough.

FOLK PREDICTIONS

- If it rains on your funeral, you will go to heaven. If it rains on your wedding, it means either good luck or there will be tears in your marriage. (Both were used!)

- If you want to "water witch" to discover water, you must use a peach tree branch.

- If a "heart cherry" tree blooms in the fall, someone close to you will die.

- If a bird picks at the window of your home, someone in the house will die.

WEATHER FOLK BELIEFS

- Cows come home before a storm.

- If a maple tree does not get "butterflies" (seed pods) there will not be a good corn crop.

- When it rains and raindrops hang on the trees or clothesline after it has stopped, there will be more rain.

- When there is jackfrost on the ground, you will get rain to wash it off again.

- If there is thunder and lightning in January, there will not be a good corn crop.

- If it rains when the sun is shining, it will rain the same time the next day.

- The weather on the first twelve days of the year will predict what the weather will be like for each of the twelve months in that year.

- If it rains for two days before and two days after a full moon, it will be wet the rest of the month.

- When blackbirds flock, it will get very cold.

- If the sparrows are not making nests, the winter is not over.

- If ants build high anthills, there will be a heavy rain.

- If the wheat ripens with the full moon, it will be a good crop.

- When you hear the "fresh" three times, you're past a frost. (These are tree frogs, and are called "fresh" in German).

- Plant corn when the grape leaves are as big as a squirrel's ear.

When digging posts for a fence, if you dig away from the full moon you won't have enough ground (there won't be enough ground around the post afterwards.) If you dig towards the full moon, you will have more than you need to place the post.

—Sandra Dannehold, St. Louis, Missouri

My wife's grandmother, Alice Howard, was a lovely, extremely intelligent person and a true lady. She was also a strong Roman Catholic who was a lay member of the Discalced Carmelites. Grandma was a very upright, moral person. One of her favorite sayings, which she used on many, many occasions, was, "Your reputation is like a white dress; once it gets stained, it can never be restored to its original beauty." She was not without a sense of humor, however. Along those same lines she would quip, "A pregnancy takes 9 months but the first one can come anytime." Another 'Grandma Howardism' referred to people finding mates: "There is never a stick so crooked that you can't find one to match." She died in 1986, but we remember her always through her folklore.

My mother-in-law, June Howard Stuhlman, had a wildly funny and offbeat sense of humor. She and her first husband, Roger, who died very young, enjoyed bantering so much, the expressions stuck with the whole family. We still say, as they did, whenever they departed: "We're off like a cheap toupee in a windstorm." And when she was teasing and being teased, her favorite retort was "You S**t!" Sometimes it devolved into "S**t on a stick." When she felt the teasing was going on too long she would always say, "Quit the horse assing around."

June died in 1999, but I remember her words, taunts, retorts, and expressions as if she were still here. In fact, we still use them all the time.

—D. James (Jim) Moses, St. Louis, Missouri

My grandmother was folklore unto herself. We still remember her sayings and expressions and superstitions and I guess we believe much of the latter. For suitcase she always said "grip," and it was "pocketbook" for purse. A vest was a "weskit." Her refrigerator was always an "icebox," which my mother continued to say, as well as my brothers and I still do. The living room was her "front room."

On New Year's Eve she would always hold paper money in one hand and with the other hand would eat the pickled herring—always done at midnight to make sure she would be rich someday. And she always placed a penny in every window to ensure that she would be rich the next year.

She pronounced house as "harse," sundae as "sunduh," "sodee" for soda, and "zink" for sink. And when she wanted to make a point or moral she could end a speech with a saying: "God helps those who help themselves." "You were born poor and you'll die poor." "You have to know somebody in this world in order to get anything." "You'll get "toe-shus" in the "boe-shus" if you eat that too much." "You can't have your cake and eat it too."

On Christmas Eve morning we all had to go to Grandma's house so that my parents, or rather Santa, could decorate the Christmas tree. My dad even had train displays every year. Then about 5 p.m. he would pick us all up at Grandma's house—including Grandma—and bring us home. We had to come in through the back door, and when opening the kitchen door, about to come in, there was always a whistle or a whistle-like sound. That was Santa rounding up his elves to take off so that we wouldn't see any of them.

For Easter celebration we did "egg butting," which some people call "nicking," to see who could have the last egg to crack. That would be good luck. And we always had an Easter egg hunt inside the house. There was always one place that delighted me the most; I thought it was a special place for eggs. Our mailbox was built into the wall and about 15 inches deep. There would always be an egg in there. When I finally learned that there really was no Easter Bunny, I was sad, but a greater loss was to know that the bunny was no longer going to put eggs in the mailbox!

I remember celebrating St. Nick's Day on December 6. We would all wake up to one of our own socks he filled every year for us. There was always a candy cane, an orange, and a small item, like a coloring book or crayons. My brother usually got a piece of wood in his stocking. St. Nick had to punish somebody to keep the tradition alive.

—Darlene Huber, St. Louis, Missouri

On Christmas Eve at my husband's grandmother's house we always played and still do, "Rob Your Neighbor." The game involves cheap gifts and dice. If you roll a double you get to pick a present and then when all the presents are picked you continue to play for a period of time and rob your neighbor of the present. It was something everyone from three to 83 could participate in and still enjoy today.

We participated in our share of crosses over door frames for good luck, burying the dried palms from Palm Sunday during a storm to protect our house, never walking under a ladder, and if we spilled salt we always threw some over our left shoulder.

When we had a house for sale in the family, we always buried a statue of St. Joseph in the front yard facing away from the house. It has worked every time we did it.

As to family folk beliefs, I had an aunt who threw a knife out the back door when it was storming and lightning. She always told us the lightning would follow the steel. So when it stopped raining we would, of course, clear the yard of the knives.

My father's language was curious in that he spoke five languages and was very precise in English, but he always would "wrench out his cup," or "put it in the zink," or go to the "houspital." These words became part of our folk vocabulary as habit even though we know they are incorrect.

"For Easter we always had, and I always make, pashka. It's a sweet cottage cheese that is served decorated with prunes, almonds and flowers. For Christmas we always have a Kringle, a sweet circular stollen made with different fillings and popular among Germans. It's a tradition for us.

A real family lore has to do with toilet training of sorts. Our son had severe constipation as a small child. As he was attempting to complete the task I would try to distract him by making him laugh. I would push on his head to help him go "number two." Our granddaughter has the same ritual during her potty training and the same pushing on her head must be done to her teddy bear also.
    —Jim and Pat Cook, St. Louis, Missouri

Our family remembers and talks all the time about the street vendors who pushed carts all through the streets selling their wares. And they all had distinctive "hollers" or "cries" to accompany their sale. "Straw—b e r r e e e s"—very drawn out and melodic was one of our favorites. The man selling clothes props would sing his product out loud and I always thought he was selling "pork chops." And I wondered if he had them hanging on the old wooden stick he was carrying. We use this now whenever we misunderstand something . . . "are you saying pork chops??" Hot tamales tasted the best from the street man walking past our house, and Sam the Watermelon Man had the best watermelons every summer. He is still the standard every summer when we buy a ripe one; and he has never been beaten by any other watermelons!

Oh, and my grandfather was the last lamplighter to live in the city. He lived on Linton Avenue and lit all the street lights and then returned in the morning to put them out. His work was distinctive and he had lots of friends made during his rounds.

I remember the Easter egg hunts in O'Fallon Park every year. And I remember the wine my grandfather made every year. The fumes throughout the two-story flat were enough to make everyone feel good.

It's memories like these which make us talk about yesterday and compare. The memories are vivid, and it's fun to pass these stories on to my kids and grandkids.

—Betty (Boots) Gassel, St. Louis, Missouri

Folk games were, perhaps, the most important part of growing up for my kids. Wiffle balls are manufactured, of course, but the way in which the game is played is, I think, pure folk imagination. It always was a game where age and skill didn't seem to matter. Everyone could play. A field could be made almost anywhere. And the Wiffle ball was a plastic sphere with holes in it; the bat was plastic. Many a tree "ate" our kids' Wiffle balls just like Charlie Brown's kite. Sometimes hitting one over the fence was an out, other times a home run—depended if the neighbors were home or not! Some finesse was required in hitting this plastic ball. But the equipment was always fully used up by the end of summer. So every Easter basket for years included a Wiffle ball in anticipation of the folk game of the summer.

—Carla Maasen, Huntsville, Alabama, formerly of St. Louis

Just in these few samples of family lore, there is folk vocabulary, folk pronunciation, folk games, superstitions, education, proverbs, holiday lore, rituals, traditions, customs, folk foods, folk occupations, supernatural legends, formulaic expressions, and family-specific lore.

Importantly, these folk texts are not only remembered, but they are still practiced or talked about or remembered in conversation or, most traditionally, fondly recounted in private, where they become the personal past, the history that is worth remembering and then following, following, following!

CHAPTER 9

ST. LOUIS FOLK FOODS
"MAULL'S ST. PAUL'S"

ONE OF THE INTERESTING INTERDISCIPLINARY METHODS OF RESEARCHING the folklore of an area is through the foods that are consumed, created, modified, or made distinctive from the resources unique to the area. Very often a regional food becomes a national food choice, but always maintaining its roots in the region where it originated. And in the latter case there is always the popular belief that it can never be prepared well except in the area where it was born. Boston baked beans and Boston cream pie are always best consumed in Massachusetts, as the belief is interpreted. And Southern fried chicken is just that—no other region compares to what Southerners can do with chicken. Buffalo wings revolve around the same lore. Each region, more states, and even more cities can lay claim to some folk food that is uniquely theirs. The argument may be specious; the facts may be distorted; the primary documents may be missing. But these minor things do not stop the "invented-here-created-here" phenomenon.

Doubt is a very clear component of how folk foods can be defined. But there are examples in which the food is clearly from one region, simply because no other place prepares it. And it can be eaten only in one identifiable place.

St. Louis has many foods from the latter category in its rich folk history. The watershed folk foods of the 1904 World's Fair have given a strong historical impetus to the identification of what is uniquely St. Louis fare. There is much "folk" doubt as to the origins expressed in these areas with a very strong civic pride. Most of them are based on food legends with different versions and for which the exact truth cannot be known. This is the charm and the romanticism of the study. All of this adds to the significance of foods and what they can reflect about a region. In fact, St. Louis has been dubbed "the mother of fast foods in America."

ST. LOUIS FOLK FOODS, SOME STILL REGIONAL, SOME WORLD FAMOUS

TOASTED RAVIOLI

Toasted ravioli is arguably the most famous folk food produced in St. Louis. The different versions of its origins are a perfect folk legend, but fortunately, they all remain within the St. Louis area.

Ravioli, as most everyone knows, is pillow-shaped pasta filled with beef, pork, veal, or a combination of the three. Today even cheeses, seafood, or vegetables stuff the pasta. Originally, however, the meat filling was the definitive ravioli.

In the southwest city section of St. Louis known as The Hill, where immigrants from northern Italy first immigrated, there are many nationally known Italian restaurants. It was in this region, as the story goes, in 1943, at the Oldani's restaurant, where Chef Terry Hill accidentally dropped one of the freshly made ravioli into a pot of hot grease. The result was a "fried ravioli," and, as the cliché goes, the rest was food history.

But another legend states that at Angelo's on The Hill, now the famous Charlie Gitto's restaurant, another chef, coincidentally named Oldani, made the same fortunate mistake and "discovered" toasted ravioli.

And finally, a third legend has it that the chef at Mama Campisi's Restaurant, also on The Hill, invented the food.

The stories are pure descriptive lore and very representative. And the claims are still being challenged, tested, and championed—but to no avail, because toasted ravioli has now become synonymous with St. Louis.

They are breaded with a special breading mix—depending on the restaurant or manufacturer—deep fried in oil, and served with marinara sauce for dipping. And they are sold everywhere in St. Louis restaurants and bars, from the diner to the upscale restaurant. And tony New York City also serves them in some restaurants because St. Louis chefs have brought culinary skills to the "Big Apple."

It's the reactions of visitors to St. Louis that identifies toasted ravioli as the real folk food, however. Their surprise, expression of disbelief, distaste, smugness, or even parochialism has greeted the little fried pillow pastas. But St. Louis cares only that it was invented here, defines part of our culture, and is delicious.

ST. LOUIS PIZZA

Next to the hamburger, pizza may be the most American of foods. No matter that Naples, Italy, claims the first pizza, Americans made it better . . . as they do in everything. But which American city has the best pizza? Now that is another debate on folk foods, all good for the research. Chicago and New York are mentioned most often as the "best," with their very different and distinct types, but St. Louis has a special version that gives the traditional varieties a strong competitor.

Imo's Pizza is widely and strongly considered to be the creator of St. Louis–style pizza.

Started in 1964 by Ed Imo, a tile contractor and installer by day, Imo's has grown to be the largest pizza chain, by far, in St. Louis, and one of the largest independent pizza parlors in the United States. And what a folk food their pizza is!

The uniqueness of Imo's pizza starts with the crust. There is no yeast in it. It is cracker-like in its consistency, and therefore very thin. The sauce is tomato-based with heavier doses of oregano than others, and the cheese is really not a cheese: provel is the name.

Imo wanted to have a cheese that did not leave strings like mozzarella; he wanted a clean bite. So he processed cheddar, Swiss, and provolone cheeses to make his provel. The folklore has it that no such cheese exists today, but the resulting taste was spectacular, and St Louis–style pizza was born.

But Imo did not stop there. He did not cut the round pieces into "pie" triangles, but sliced the pizza into three to four inch squares just as if he were cutting the tile he laid by day. There is no folding of his pizza; that's for "New Yawkers" and their mozzarella. So when visitors come to St. Louis to taste a pizza and they try Imo's, the folk food arguments begin again and again.

Today Imo's has branched out into a few other midwestern states and advertises itself always as St. Louis–style pizza! The style has become so characteristic that provel cheese, manufactured in Wisconsin exclusively for Imo's, can now be bought, packaged, in St. Louis markets.

ST. PAUL SANDWICH

This Chinese food—yes, Chinese sandwich—is distinctly St. Louis, identified nationally as such, and a destination food for many visitors.

The origins, in true folk style, are unclear, but we do know that Chinese-American restaurants in St. Louis have been making these sandwiches for years. Sometimes they are labeled as "egg-foo-young" dinners, but the sandwich remains the same.

It starts with an egg foo young patty, which is made of some ground meat (beef, pork, or lamb), bean sprouts, and some diced onions. Dill pickle slices must be added, along with tomatoes, lettuce, and mayonnaise and all placed between two slices of white bread—which must be Wonder Bread! Legend has it that a St. Louis Chinese dinette tried to improve the sandwich by using hamburger buns and sold nothing!

Very popular sandwich, obscure origins, identified with a region—here are the elements of a perfect folk food. Add one more: A few Chinese restaurants in San Francisco have added the sandwich to their menus.

But what about the name? Start your own legend here, but some say the creator was raised in St. Paul, Minnesota; or was devoted to the saint; or wanted to make an American-sounding dish to make more money with a sandwich that is not typically Chinese fare; or one Chinese chef experimented with a customer's wishes. Choose one and you have a folktale of St. Louis foods.

PORK STEAKS

Mention pork steaks to anyone in any part of the country outside of St. Louis and people think you are joking. They are just unheard of. But St. Louis loves its barbequed pork steaks.

Taken from the shoulder of the hog, the pork steaks are grilled most originally on an open pit, after a time placed in a roasting pan filled with barbeque sauce with some beer poured in to tenderize the meat, and then left to simmer for a time until very tender. There are other methods to prepare the meat, also, and each one, of course, is the best! It is the most popular meat item in St. Louis for barbeques during the summer, and even restaurants have added them to their menus. Church picnics and festivals even revolve around pork steaks for the main dinner at the fair.

But visitors are still skeptical!

THE SLINGER

Other places in the United States may have "slingers" for breakfast, but St. Louisans will fight to the death in their claim that the slinger was invented here.

Edmonds chili is a St. Louis tradition in itself, but some diners used it in creative ways to develop the Slinger. A concoction most often associated with breakfast, it consists of the following: two eggs, prepared any way, hash browns, a hamburger patty, all mixed up or placed side by side and covered with chili. Sometimes a tamale with cheese and onions is topped on the chili to make what is dubbed a "Quality" one.

Some informants report that they eat one of these daily on their way to work. Some love Slingers as a luncheon meal; others make a dinner out of it. But two additional notes are important here: (1) folklore has it that Slingers are best enjoyed after midnight, on the way home from a night out; and (2), the antacid, Tums, was invented in St. Louis. Is there a folk connection here?

MAULL'S BARBECUE SAUCE

Louis Maull began his grocery business on a horse-drawn wagon in St. Louis in 1897. Then, in 1905, he established the Louis Maull Cheese and Fish Company, selling his products to restaurants, grocery stores, and wholesalers. About ten years after starting the Cheese and Fish Company, he began mixing tomatoes, anchovies, and peppers to be used as a sauce or "gravy" for various meats. In 1926, this mixture became the barbeque sauce that bore his name and finally the only product he marketed. It became a household word in St. Louis homes: Don't baste your Bar-B-Q! Maull it! No pork steak worth its considerable fat was made without Maull's.

The typical St. Louis barbeque sauce

is tomato based, thinned with vinegar, and has a sweet and spicy combination of ingredients. In itself, it has become a folk food very different from other cities.

An interesting sideline: St. Louis is the world leader in per capita consumption of barbeque sauce! Everyone has been completely "Maulled."

BEVO

The name, rather than the beverage, remains a St. Louis tradition today. The Bevo Mill, a south St. Louis landmark, is still standing and houses a restaurant famous for its German cuisine. And the expression, "down by the Bevo," is known by all St. Louisans as a directional icon and famous meeting place.

In 1916, Anheuser-Busch began making a nonalcoholic malt beverage when beer was forbidden to American soldiers. In 1919, when Prohibition began, the product became so popular that the brewery was making almost 5 million cases annually. And the "near beer" was called "Bevo," which was a corruption of the Slavic term for beer, "pivo."

Here folk cultures collided to produce a new folk term for a beverage and eventually a very recognizable St. Louis word for a restaurant, a neighborhood, and a meeting place. And folk vocabulary went even further, becoming American slang: a young, very inexperienced officer in the army was called a "Bevo," after the beverage from St. Louis.

And in another curious way, Anheuser-Busch used the French folk tale character, Renard the Fox, as its mascot and advertising symbol. Friezes, featuring the Fox dressed in his distinctive folk costume, decorate Bevo Mill and the Bevo building at the brewery even today.

The beverage may no longer be manufactured, but the name lives on in several folklore forms.

MAYFAIR HOTEL SALAD DRESSING

In 1925, the Mayfair Hotel, now the Roberts Mayfair Hotel and a beautiful example of a boutique hostelry, introduced a salad dressing recognized as St. Louis's contribution to the world of salads. The development of the dressing has all the elements of a legend: The recipe is known only to the chef, who passes it on to his succeeding chef, who then does the same after he retires—and always only one person knows the recipe, and "under penalty of death" can never reveal it to anyone.

Legend continues that people have sneaked into the kitchen of the hotel, which was a former speakeasy, by the way, to spy on the chef preparing the dressing. But the security was so tight that no one ever managed to steal the secret. The flavor of the dressing and what makes it special continues to intrigue. It is an egg-based dressing mixed with oil and seasoned with anchovies, garlic, prepared mustard, celery, black peppercorns, onions, and champagne.

The speculation begins: Is it the champagne that makes the difference? What kind is used? What kind of mustard? No, it must be the anchovies! Legends are made of such curiosity, but the romance of the dressing continues with no one knowing the secret.

TED DREWES FROZEN CUSTARD

"It really is good, guys!" So goes the byline of Ted Drewes in his television commercials throughout St. Louis media. The man himself has become a St. Louis folk legend, and the custard stand an icon—especially the one (of two) located on the historic Route 66.

In 1929, Ted's father developed frozen custard—which is *not* ice cream, thank you. Its custard is made with egg yolks and mixed with less air than ice cream and has at least 10 percent butterfat. But when the lines outside his store overflow into the traffic on the Old Route 66, and it's close to midnight (!), who's thinking of butterfat? Ted Drewes *is* the summer happening in St. Louis. The place for dessert after any meal! The place to meet anyone and everyone! The place to be a paparazzi victim or celebrity!

There are only two stands, both in the city of St. Louis and both on the south side. But the one on Route 66 draws the crowds. Requests over the years begging to franchise his product have been declined over

and over again. To Ted Drewes, this is St. Louis, and this is a pure product that would be diluted if spread around so haphazardly. He and his folk food are one identity known nationally.

Drewes has also added a folk vocabulary to the mix. His "concrete" offering—a shake so thick that you can turn it upside down, as the clerk does for effect—and it will not fall out—is a pure St. Louis folk expression. And the ways to flavor the concrete are endless—nuts, butterscotch, chocolate chips, cherries, hot fudge, devil's food cake, pistachio nuts, peanut butter, pumpkin pie—whatever. Each has a special significance in its folk name, many of which depict St. Louis: the Dutchman, the nickname of a high school mascot in St. Louis, which in itself is a folk appellation; or the Terramizzou, representing The Hill and the familiar name of the University of Missouri.

GUS' PRETZELS

Pretzel legends in folklore are legion. The most popular one relates the story of Catholic monks who invented the pretzel to resemble the hands crossed over the breast in a praying gesture. The configuration, with its resultant three circles, further symbolized the Trinity and became a constant reminder of the need for prayer through the appearance of food.

That's the shape of a pretzel most Americans recognize, when in the bread or baked variety. But in St. Louis, it's the pretzel stick! And Gus' Pretzels, an icon in St. Louis, developed the famous pretzel to resemble a breadstick. This was in 1920, and almost one hundred years later, the company is still family owned, serves four hundred customers a day, and makes more than nine thousand pretzels weekly.

Most importantly, Gus' Pretzels is a pure form of folklore. It was passed down through generations, uses the same recipe, develops variations, like cinnamon-sugar, and even sandwiches like the hot dog, bratwurst, or salsiccia encased in the famous pretzel dough. In the same location since it was founded, Gus' is directly across from Anheuser-Busch Brewery on the city's south side. The aroma from the pretzel bakery mixing with the brewing beer creates an instant marketing ad.

Even street vendors sell the simple product: bread stick pretzels, peeking out of a brown paper bag tempting drivers stopping at traffic signals. And these vendors don't even work for Gus'; they simply buy the pretzels on their own because they know they have a recognizable product and a ready market in the regional familiarity with Gus'.

For fifty cents, the golden brown pretzel, crispy and crunchy on the outside and warm and chewy on the inside, perhaps dipped in various mustards or cheese, serves as a meal for hundreds of St. Louisans daily. Folk beliefs have even developed around Gus' product: for a hangover dip the pretzel in their raspberry mustard for a certain cure; or, at Easter or Christmas, bread must always be broken with pretzels from Gus' to transfer the good luck of a long and a happy life which Gus' has enjoyed; or on a wedding anniversary or a birthday, have a pretzel baked into the year being celebrated and everyone must partake in the sharing in order to have the magic of contagion. Good luck will transfer to all involved.

St. Louis rejects Philly pretzels and New York's trendy bread basket pretzels as imposters. They are convinced they have the best in Gus' and the whole body of folklore testifies to their claim.

CRAB RANGOON

Cream cheese is not usually a product used in China to make a dish. Crab Rangoon was born in St. Louis and for the most part has stayed here. These are best described as deep-fried dumplings stuffed with cream cheese, crab meat, and scallions. Wrapped in Chinese wonton wrappers and molded into a triangle shape or sometimes a flower shape, these appetizers were apparently named after Rangoon, the former capital of Burma (now Myanmar). And, they also have been rumored to have been invented at the 1904 St. Louis World's Fair, where they received a popular welcome and have never left. These folk origins add a mysterious quality to these dumplings and make them special St. Louis folk foods.

THE AMIGHETTI SPECIAL

Some cities call it the hobo, or the submarine, or the poor boy, but St. Louis calls it the Amighetti's Special. Ham, roast beef, Genoa salami, brick cheese, lettuce, tomatoes, pickles, onions, and pepperocini—all basted in a special sauce and most importantly placed between two pieces of Amighetti's homemade bread. Forget the Philly cheese steak, scream St. Louisans.

Lou Amighetti, an Italian immigrant, started the bakery in 1921 in The Hill section of St. Louis. The smell of the bread in the ovens was a severe test to communicants' attention at the St. Ambrose Catholic Church directly across the street. But they knew that breakfast of bread and butter, hot and fresh, directly from the oven with the sweet creamery butter, was only minutes away.

When Amighetti added his sandwiches, the lines twisted (ironically) across the street in front of the Church, all anticipating "the St. Louis sandwich." And the folk aspect continued in the "mystery" sauce. What was in it? How was it made? Who can find out? No one has ever discovered it, and the folk food continues—only in St. Louis.

DAD'S COOKIE COMPANY

Scotland in St. Louis? It happened in 1927. The legend is that Dad's Original Scotch Oatmeal Cookies arrived in California in 1900. One of the first franchise stories in American corporate life developed. Entrepreneurs from all over the United States bought rights to the company name, way ahead of the modern franchise movement, and Carpenter's Ice Cream in north St. Louis was the proud franchisee in 1927. He discovered that the cookies were a perfect complement to St. Louis's rich butterfat ice cream. And Dad's Cookies was born and has never left. Two generations later, Dad's is still here, having been merged with Renz Bakery at the corner of Louisiana and Keokuk avenues. Here, again, is the pure folk method of passing traditions (recipes) to son and grandson. The bakery is still at the same location, and the interior itself has not changed. There are the accented antique woods, the glass display cases, and even the marble counters. Cookies are even weighed on the original bakery scale and then wrapped in a brown paper bag tied with white string. In true folklore definitions, more flavors of cookies are being offered, but the Scotch Oatmeal, still following the original pattern, are the best sellers. And in a marriage of folk foods, the 1913-established Crown Candy Kitchen soda fountain sells the cookies as complements to its 14 percent butterfat ice cream. Even St. Louis "gourmet" stores sell the cookies.

As validation of its folk food status in St. Louis, Dad's Cookie Company is the only remaining store in the United States from the approximate two dozen original franchises. It is the same recipe, made in the same bakery, in the same surroundings, and served traditionally as a part of many family celebration stories. Even the Dad's Cookies Jars have become collector's items, lending themselves to legends of their own.

RED HOT RIPLETS

Potato chips are not a St. Louis invention. They are popular, but not discovered in St. Louis. But then the Old Vienna Snack Food Company, a St. Louis–based firm, developed the Red Hot Riplets. They have become a St. Louis favorite and a national phenomenon thanks to a rapper.

The riplets are a "ridge-cut" chip that is made with a sweet and fiery hot barbeque seasoning. The label states that they are made with St. Louis–Style Hot Sauce.

St. Louisans strongly believe that these chips are the best medicine for the allergies and sinus infections that attack everyone: One bite and your head is cleared forever!

The rapper, Terry Miller, in one of his songs referred to these chips: "I need some Kool-Aid with my Red Hot Riplets." And now the world knows.

Is it a coincidence that St. Louis also leads the United States in per capita consumption of Kool-Aid?

GOOEY BUTTER CAKE

The pure St. Louis folk food dessert is the Gooey Butter Cake. It is now made by every bakery and supermarket in St. Louis. Its origin and tradition are all lore. Apparently, or as the story goes, a German baker added the wrong ingredients to a cake batter. It was runny, but very moist on the top, and the bottom was a crusty version of yellow cake dough. Result: gooey butter cake, so make the same mistake again and again!

The bottom of the cake is a yellow cake mix with a layer of butter topped with eggs, cream cheese, and powdered sugar all mixed before baking. Variants are many: chocolate, pistachio, coconut, peanut, almond, blueberry, etc. But all start with the basic gooey butter. And gourmands say that the creamier and more pudding-like the cake, the more "pure" it is, just like the mistake. National television programs on food networks have recognized the cake and have even staged contests for the best in St. Louis!

THE FOOD OF THE 1904 WORLD'S FAIR

Never has any World's Fair become as much of a research topic than the St. Louis World's Fair of 1904. Situated in Forest Park, one of the largest urban parks in the world with nearly 1,300 acres, the Fair gave St. Louis significant architecture that is still standing and used for cultural purposes, like the St. Louis Art Museum and the Bird Cage at the world-famous Saint Louis Zoo. The World's Fair Pavilion was built in 1909 from the proceeds of the Fair and remains as a beautiful and functional monument to that glorious enterprise. In song, musical comedy, and movies, especially in memories of Judy Garland, the Fair is still celebrated.

But some people remember the Fair for its contribution to American food tastes. The ice cream cone, iced tea, hot dogs on buns, and lemonade were all introduced at the Fair and have become iconic American food, right up there with apple pie.

Yet the introduction of these food products always has attendant folk tales that temper the actual origins. Again, the versions of lore, so important in its definition, surround the Fair food. Ask St. Louis residents, though, and there is no question. The city gave the world the ice cream cone (in waffle form), the bun for the hot dog, and iced tea and lemonade to wash it all down! Some even say that toasted ravioli was invented at the Fair and became the country's first finger food! That is really an old wives' tale!

FITZ'S ROOT BEER

Fitz's Root Beer, created and produced in St. Louis since 1947, is the clear choice of residents as the best root beer ever developed. With a recipe that is characteristically secret, the folks at Fitz's are open about one ingredient: pure cane sugar. This, they assert, makes their product the carefully produced, quality, tasty "beer" unique among others, anywhere.

And their root beer floats have taken on lore of their own. They are made with mounds of vanilla ice cream precariously placed on a frosted mug. The trick is to consume the float by not losing any ice cream and causing the root beer to marry it! Attempts by customers to accomplish the feat are as varied as the many proclaimed disciples of Fitz's. Sitting and watching all the attempts to "save the ice cream" has become a folk tradition.

The background for this entire "people watching" is the actual bottling process. Behind large windows in the dining room, customers can watch the root beer being mixed and bottled.

Also, Fitz's has become a gathering place for nostalgic reunions. Grandparents regularly bring their grandkids in and pass on their stories of happenings at Fitz's when they were in high school. In fact, actual high school club reunions have been held at Fitz's. The folklore is alive in this destination place!

MISCELLANEOUS ST. LOUIS FOLK FOOD TRADITIONS

The "Frozen Fishbowl" at Rigazzi's restaurant on The Hill is a thirty-two-ounce goblet of draft beer, a registered trademark that the oldest restaurant on The Hill uses as its signature. It is famous throughout the city, even becoming a folk phrase: "I'm so thirsty I cold drink two fishbowls." And everyone knows they are referring to Rigazzi's.

The Mayflower Prosperity Sandwich was invented to allay the hunger of men who had too much to drink. Sourdough bread is layered with ham, turkey, bacon, asparagus, broccoli, sharp cheddar cheese, and Parmesan cheese and then put under the broiler. The sandwich is still served at the hotel and is unique to it.

Volpi's Salumeria, founded in 1902 on The Hill, is world renowned for its prosciutto, often designated the best in the world, and bought by restaurants from all over the world. Their salami and other Italian meat products compete equally as favorites for St. Louisans to purchase. And a source no less informed than the *New York Times*, in an article about "hero" sandwiches, firmly declared that one has to have the best salami to make one—and Volpi's in St. Louis is their choice!

Fried brain sandwiches, made from the calf's brain, were a staple for many years in St. Louis taverns. Then the appearance of Mad Cow Disease buried the "brains," but some travel books still list brain sandwiches as a St. Louis tradition "to avoid."

French Onion Soup made at Famous-Barr, for decades the largest department store in St. Louis, once owned by the May Company, is St. Louis's most "famous" soup. When Macy's merged with the May Company and renamed all the Famous-Barr stores, there were even petitions circulated around St. Louis that Macy's not do away with the French Onion Soup in the restaurants! Macy's did not, and the soup is still enjoyed today, and in the folklore tradition made with a secret recipe.

For years people have passed around *the* recipe, acquired from someone who knew someone who had a connection to a cook there who was fired and wanted to get back at his employer . . . on and on and on in folklore style. But none of the recipes tastes like the original.

There's a St. Louis belief, almost a proverb, that a marriage is not legal in St. Louis unless the wedding banquet includes mostaccioli (pronounced musk-a-chol-li)! This tubular pasta, legend tells us, was not even recognizable as pasta by Italian food experts. Origins, again, are obscure, but the St. Louis Italian chefs created the pasta as a derivative of penne. The word itself, meaning "moustache," is a clue to the tale of "invented" pasta. Food historians are amused at the word and cannot confirm the origin, and certainly cannot confirm the pasta in "pasta genealogy." But it has become a form of a superstition or folk belief in St. Louis: no wedding without mostaccioli.

There are certainly other St. Louis folk food traditions that help to tell the story of the lore of the city. Crown Candy Kitchen's Heavenly Hash, Bissinger's Molasses Lollipops, Mavrakos' candy, Woofie's Hot Dogs, Carl's Hamburgers, and O. T. Hodge's chili are all tradition-based folk texts that give way to more legends, more family remembrances, and more experiences, real or imagined—perhaps even more after they are no longer produced!

CHAPTER 10

ETHNIC ST. LOUIS FOLKLORE

JEWISH, ITALIAN, AND SLAVIC— FROM CHALLAH TO PANETTONE TO POTICA TO AMERICA

IN ANY ATTEMPT TO DEFINE THE CITY OF ST. LOUIS, ONE ALWAYS encounters the argument that the city is simply, and importantly, a collection of neighborhoods based on ethnicity. Germans, Italians, Jews, Croatians, Hispanics, Irish, African-Americans, Native Americans, Polish, Bosnians, and French, among many other nationalities, had all originally settled in various parts of the region and for many years kept their traditions active but could not keep them completely pure. The American experience tempered many cultural traditions; but the roots of their cultures were always there, and the creation of the new folklore helps develop the charm of St. Louis.

Except for the area in southwest St. Louis known as The Hill, most of the neighborhoods have lost their cohesion, and the "immigrants" have assimilated throughout the metropolitan landscape. But the lore that was originally part of their culture was not lost in their moves. It was carried on by the ethnic groups, passed on traditionally to their offspring, and enhanced by the merge with other cultures and has become uniquely St. Louis.

Researching the folklore of all the ethnic groups would reveal a history of the region that could not be obtained from other sources. An awareness of diversity, a worshipping of tradition, a useful stereotyping, and a productive collaboration would be shown as the results of all the folklife created and sustained in St. Louis from all its ethnic neighborhoods.

The Jewish community, the Italian neighborhood, and the Slavic groups, especially Croatian, all have maintained and still do maintain a sense of lore that reinforces cohesiveness. These are just three examples of cultures with original lore combined with the American experience in St. Louis. But they represent all other ethnicities in the manner in which their lore functions.

Most of the examples have come from radio programs I hosted asking for ethnic lore from the St. Louis region. Other materials are from primary sources—countless interviews with the representative nationality. There are even examples from third- and fourth-generation descendants who keep the traditions alive. Personal applications of the lore are also included. My paternal grandparents came to St. Louis from the Lombardy region of Italy, and my maternal grandparents came to St. Louis from Croatia, then a part of Yugoslavia. Growing up with them gave me a primary source for ethnic lore and a real appreciation of how their life in St. Louis changed its folk application but not its spirit.

In every case, the informants were talkative, passionate, defined by their traditions, proud of their roots, open and sharing, nostalgic, and happy that the memory and performance of folklife still lives. The examples are not exhaustive but representative of the cultures. Reading each group's sample lore will reveal characteristics unique to their ethnicity but combined with other groups will show an awareness of diversity that was acceptable before its time.

JEWISH LORE
PROVERBS/SAYINGS/RETORTS

More than any other ethnic group, Jewish lore has the most connotative, ironic, and devilishly fun expressions. When they are used, there is no need to elaborate; the meaning is always clear and pertinent. They are not the dangerous threats they seem to be but are really a sarcastic poetry from a folk group that knows real pain.

- May the seven seas not be enough for your enemas.

- When God closes a door, God opens a window.

- May you be alone in paradise.

- May your buttocks fall off.

- May your nose run and your feet smell.

- May your finger get stuck in your nose.

- If you don't listen, you have to feel the pain.

- May you turn into a sparrow and owe your existence to the droppings of a horse.

- May you grow so rotten that goats, skunks, and pigs refuse to be near you.

- The sun will set without your help.

- May you never go to hell, but always be on your way.

- Everyone is kneaded out of the same dough, but not baked in the same oven.

- That all your teeth shall fall out, but one should remain for a toothache.

- You should grow old like an onion with your feet in the air and your head in the ground.

- You can't chew with someone else's teeth.

- Don't spit in the well; you might drink from it later.

- You should have a child through the ribs.

- May a band of gypsies camp in your belly and train bears to dance on your liver.

- May all your enemies move in with you.

- Corns should grow on your nose.

- He who looks finds.

- What the child says outdoors, he has learned indoors.

- If you want to go from one room to another you have to use your feet.

- If the rich could hire someone to die for them the poor would make a nice living.

JEWISH FOLK MEDICINE

- To remove a wart, use duct tape.

- For a toothache, place a dry tea bag over the pain.

- Eat a raw clove of garlic for a cold.

- Hot water and lemon first thing in the morning will lead to a long life.

- Rub buttermilk on freckles to get rid of them.

- Chicken soup *always* cures or prevents a cold.

- Apply cornstarch mixed with Vaseline to cure diaper rash.

- Eat a teaspoon of Vick's Vapo-Rub every three hours to cure a cold.

- When breastfeeding her baby, the woman must drink lots of beer to ensure a healthy child.

- Goose grease plastered on a chest will cure bronchitis.

- Rub a wart with a peeled potato. When the potato rots the wart will disappear.

- A bag of hot cornmeal applied to the head can relieve a headache.

JEWISH FOLK VOCABULARY

The Jewish culture has contributed many Yiddish words to the American vocabulary. They are not specifically related to St. Louis, of course, but their usage is not diminished by their national appeal. *Mazel tov, mensch, schlemiel, oy vey!, kosher, schmear, chatchke, schlemazel, meshugge, kvetch, schlep, klutz, schmaltz, tuchus,* and *chutzpa,* among others, need no translations. As words they are adopted by every folk group and are even used more extensively in longer folk texts. They have embedded themselves into the American culture as strong contributions of the Jewish community.

ITALIAN LORE
PROVERBS/SAYINGS/RETORTS

- The liar needs a good memory.

- Since the house is on fire, let's get warm!

- Always marry a woman from your own neighborhood.

- Life's too short; don't worry!

- Give them a finger and they'll take the arm.

- To every pigeon, his own nest is the best.

- Who sleeps doesn't catch the fish.

- Those who make themselves sheep will be eaten by the wolf.

- The trouble that affects everyone is only half trouble.

- Bed is the poor man's opera.

- A small cask makes a very good wine.

- He doesn't have hairs on his tongue! (He says what he feels.)

- When one Pope dies, they make another.

- It happens as often as the death of a Pope. (A rare occurrence)

- May the wolf die. (Used to wish someone good luck before an important undertaking.)

- He's lucky. His wine bottle is full and his wife is drunk.

- She's always as good as bread.

- God makes them, and then he mates them. (Used when it's hard to understand two people in a relationship.)

- Speak to me outside of your teeth. (Don't hold back; give it to me straight.)

- You can laugh today, but tomorrow it's my turn.

- There are no roses without thorns.

- True friends are as rare as white flies.

- An egg today is better than a hen tomorrow.

ITALIAN EXPRESSIONS: FLIP YOUR CHIN!

It is often said that if an Italian had his hands tied behind his back he would not be able to talk. Flamboyant gestures, hand signs, and facial moves are the nonverbals of folklore that need no definition. Each culture that uses them speaks the proverbial volumes to each other. They are not learned in a formal setting, but by acculturation. No ethnic group is more identified with folk gestures than the Italians. They are ideal informal learning, used traditionally, and say exactly what the "speaker" wants to say. The meaning behind each gesture is not specific to a region. But the gestures of the Italian conversations have contributed everyday expressions to the American idiom. When something is B.S., or someone "flipped the bird," or the "evil eye" is planted, or the fist is raised dramatically, the words follow from the gestures. Italians employ the gestures in a clever economic transmission of their lore. And the transmission becomes vocal expressions for other cultures.

ITALIAN FOLK MEDICINE AND FOLK BELIEFS

When someone is ill, boil holy water. Then put extra virgin olive oil in the water. If the oil moves in a certain shape, determined to be good by the one who pours the oil, then the person will be okay.

Boil extra virgin olive oil, let it cool, and then put a few drops in the ear for an earache (especially good for babies).

During a severe thunderstorm, burn the palm from Palm Sunday. You must use a white candle, collect the ashes over a bowl, say three Hail Mary's, and then throw the ashes into the storm. No harm will come to your household.

When someone is sick, the evil eye obviously got them. One must place a broom behind the door of the sick person. And at night when the evil eye returns to claim his prey, curiosity forces him to stop and count the broom straws. By the time he is finished, it will be daylight and he must run for fear of people seeing him. Sometimes a bag of rice is used, and the evil spirit must count the grains before he claims his prize. The same result will occur.

- A glass of red wine, boiled and then drunk as hot as one can stand it, will cure a cold.

- Rub the chest with olive oil to cure a cold.

- Rub the head with olive oil to cure baldness.

- Use the boiled red onion skins from making the Easter eggs to cure a fever. Use them as a poultice.

- Wear a copper bracelet to cure rheumatism.

- Garlic placed under the armpits will reduce a high fever.

- Always eat the crust of the bread to have a full head of hair.

- Tie a string around a wart to cure it.

- To cure diarrhea, eat fried eggs at every meal.

- Carry an onion in your pocket and you'll never have a fever.

- Chamomile tea is used to treat boils, cure stomach aches, relieve menstrual cramps, or cure insomnia.

- Stick the sharp end of the palm from Palm Sunday into a stye to cure it.

- Gold rubbed over a boil or stye will rid it from the body.

- Place a rosemary plant near the front door to ward off evil. It is believed that the Virgin Mary, on her way to Bethlehem to give birth to the Christ child, dropped her shawl, and when she picked it up, beautiful scented rosemary was growing in the same spot.

- After someone has visited you uninvited, sweep the room clean and out the door through which the visitor arrived to avoid bad luck.

- Never eat mushrooms gathered under a full moon. They will cause sickness and maybe death.

- Throw salt, the coarser the better, at the front doorsill of your new home to deter the evil spirits.

SLAVIC (CROATIAN)
SAYINGS/PROVERBS

- If sorrow would not talk, it would die.
- If strokes are good to get, they are good to receive.
- Make mountains out of molehills.
  (*Proviti od muhe slona.*)
- Too much midwife, a lazy child.
  (*Puvo baba, kilavo dijete.*)
- The big thieves handle the little ones.
- The believer is happy; the doubter is wise.
- Speak the truth, then leave quickly.
- Pray to God, but keep rowing to the shore.
- If you want to sing you can always find a song.
- A dog has friends because he wags his tail instead of his tongue.
- A good rest is half the work.
- Tell the truth and shame the Devil.
- If envy would burn, there would be no need for wood.
- One ounce of luck is better than a pound of brains.
- Don't go selling the hide while the bear remains in the hole.
- Men wish, but God decides.
- You have bigger eyes than your stomach.
  (*Imat veci oci od zeluca.*)
- When willows bear grapes. (Never will happen)
- Don't buy a cat in a bag.
  (*Ne jupuj macka u vreci.*)
- A suit doesn't make a man.
- Sweep the ground in front of your own door.
  (*Pocisti provo pred svojum vratima.*)
- One hand washes the other.
  (*Ruka ruku mije.*)
- If you dig a hole under someone else, you'll fall into it yourself.

- In lies, one has short legs.

- Hasten very slowly.
  (*Zuri polako.*)

- The way it came is the way it will go.
  (*Kaka doslo, take proslo.*)

- In trouble you can find a hero.

- A disaster never comes alone.
  (*Nesreca nikad ne dolazi sama.*)

- The one who is well fed does not believe the hungry man.

- If you ask, you don't have to wander.
  (*Tkopita, ne skita.*)

SLAVIC (CROATIAN) FOLK MEDICINE AND FOLK BELIEFS

- When visiting someone, always bring a gift. It should be food or drink and never yellow flowers.

- Thirteen of anything is bad luck.

- Don't greet visitors or friends with a kiss or handshake over the doorstep. That will be bad luck. Always go inside and give your greeting.

- If a woman just had a baby, never visit her at night.

- If you have a bad cough, drink a beer right before going to bed.

- Take *pelinkovac*, plum brandy, for cure of stomach aches.

- To cure hiccups, rub a mixture of vinegar and mustard on your tongue. Hold for three minutes.

- Add salt and pepper to two shots of plum brandy to cure an upset stomach.

- If a bird hits the window, someone in the house will die.

- Do not put your keys on the table; you'll lose money.

- Never show a baby to a stranger until the baby is at least forty days old.

- Never cut your hair when someone in your family is unhealthy.

- Never give anyone an even number of flowers. Even numbers are for the dead.

- Don't cut your hair during a pregnancy. It will sap the strength from the baby.

- For a sore throat, make a mixture of mashed garlic and water. Then gargle.

- New clothes washed on the full moon will not wear well.

- Hearing an owl hoot at noon is a sign of death.

- Hearing a dog howl at night is a sign of death.

- Never allow a pregnant woman to do any work by raising her hands above her head. This will tie the umbilical cord around the baby's neck and the baby will die.

THE COMMON THREAD: BREAD

There is a distinct folklore surrounding the use of bread through-out most cultures. Folk speech, foodways, superstitions, proverbs—all verbal lore is replete with references to the "staff of life." In many forms of the lore, bread has magical power, even mythological begin-nings, and is at the very center of the folk culture. In some cultures, bread symbolizes human dignity and is often worn as clothing in pro-testing human rights.

The Jewish, Italian, and Slavic (Croatian) cultures represented in St. Louis ethnicities, not surprisingly, can be connected by bread in dif-ferent forms but used in traditional folk ways. Generations of a culture have followed the breaking of its ethnic bread and even baked it without the written recipe. The "folk" way of baking by sight and feel adds a dimension of connectivity to each of them.

For the Jewish community, challah is the special egg bread usually reserved for the Sabbath. It also refers to the bread that was set aside for the high priests in the Temple of Jerusalem. When made, challah can be braided, or made ladder-like or even circular, which signified a desire for a long life. Tradition requires that when the dough for challah is made, and before it is allowed to rise, a small part of it must be torn off and burned as a reminder of the offerings to the Temple. It is used in this folk expression as a replacement for the sacrificial offerings.

Oftentimes there are two loaves of challah lined up on a table before cutting to remember the Temple, where two breads were lined up before the altar. Then the breads are cut after the blessing is given. Challah is a uniting force, a traditional symbol for centuries, and a folk tradition used in many ways of folklife.

For Italians, bread is perhaps the most significant part of any meal. From eating it by breaking it in pieces, without the benefit of a knife, to dipping it in the tomato sauce left on the plate, it serves as the one folk food link that makes every meal special. It is not just the consuming of the bread, but in the most significant way, the breaking of the bread of family, friendship, community, good luck, contagious magic, and fellowship.

Panettone, a distinctive, round, cupola-shaped loaf of bread, is the Italian version of a specific folk food. Taken from the Italian word, *panetto*, meaning "a small loaf of bread," or *pal de ton*, meaning "bread of luxury," the bread was developed in Milan hundreds of years ago. Immigrants from this Lombardy region of northern Italy who came to St. Louis are said to have brought the bread with them.

The reason for the name of the bread itself is an example of folk versions, making panettone a special folk food. And there are legends surrounding its very origin—almost creating a mythology.

It seems that a nobleman, Atellani, in fifteenth-century Milan, fell in love with Adalgisa, the daughter of a poor baker named Toni. To claim her hand in marriage, the rich nobleman disguised himself as a baker and developed light, creamy, rich bread filled with raisins, candied lemon peels, and orange peels. This special, delicious loaf of bread convinced the baker that the nobleman loved his daughter. And the marriage was held with da Vinci himself in attendance. The bread, of course, was served at the wedding and given the name *Pan del Ton*, or Toni's bread.

A folk food, panettone, begins in legend, cements a marriage, is named for a baker who did not make it, and is traditionally produced centuries later. Folklore is alive. Christmas time, panettone, shaped like a dome of a cathedral such as the Duomo in Milan and filled with candied fruits, is a *must* food to be eaten at every Italian celebration.

Even folk beliefs have developed along with the bread: The bread with all the "gifts" baked inside represents the Three Wise Men's gifts to the Baby Jesus. Some say the shape of the bread is the shape of the manger where Jesus was born. Others believe that the bread must be eaten only with hot cocoa for good luck. Others practice saving a piece of the Christmas bread to place under the pillow during the twelve days of Christmas so that good luck will follow them all the year long.

Panettone, like challah, is a uniting force. Its various applications have become part of the lore of St. Louis and other cities at Christmas time. Giving the panettone as a gift references the belief that the recipient will never go hungry, that the blessings of Christmas will be transferred to him or her, and that the Italian bread tradition will become a part of the larger culture.

Potica (po-tee-sa), from *poviti*, "to roll up," known by many other names in Slavic culture, is a rich, thinly rolled sweet bread dough, filled with a sweet, very moist, crushed walnut filling. Very often shaped like a strudel, it has survived hundreds of years of Slavic lore.

Potica, too, is special bread made for important occasions and holidays, primarily Christmas and Easter. It also serves as the bond among the family members eating the meal together and enjoying this special bread as a treat. Often the baker adds her own special touch to the bread, such as raisins, or currants, even some chocolate, creating a folk definition in itself. But the baker makes certain that the important people in her life get a taste of the bread so that the abundance, signified by the rich filling, can be shared as a magic of transference.

Often too, potica, is taken to church at Christmas or Easter so that it can be blessed by the priest and thereby ensure that the people partaking of the bread will have good luck. If the bread is made for a wedding, it is important for the bride and groom to cut the bread themselves, as with a wedding cake, so that good fortune will follow.

One legend has it that the many layers of the potica represent the levels of abundance that a person will receive when he eats it. Many layers with much filling are not only a mark of a good baker but can mean a lot in a folk belief and tradition. Finally, potica has also entered the mainstream culture with different ingredients in the same basic recipe. Bakeries all over the United States manufacture it and ship it year-round. But its roots are in ethnic lore and made meaningful by the American experience.

So folk groups have maintained their identity through folk traditions and folkways. But they have made a significant difference in the American understanding of the lore. As in St. Louis, where the Jewish, Italian, and Slavic communities have been significant, the lore has become integral to the character of the city. It has helped define it, value it, and make it a much richer culture.

CHAPTER 11

ANOTHER ETHNICITY
THE ST. LOUIS GERMANS AND *ÜBER* FOLKLORE

WHEN IT IS CONSIDERED THAT IMMIGRANT LORE, BROUGHT TO THE UNITED States and tweaked by the American experience, becomes a different lore on the basis of experiences, none can be more applicable than the German folklife in St. Louis. Other nationalities, as has been noted, have certainly left their mark on the lore of St. Louis, but the German influence through immigration was so completely assimilated into the St. Louis culture that it became identified, in many ways, with native folklore. German vocabulary, proverbs, superstitions, foods, religious legends, and other forms of folklore became the basis for what is described as the "American" lore of St. Louis, so great was the contribution of the German community to the St. Louis region.

Lured to St. Louis by emigration societies in Germany that described St. Louis as the "American Rhineland," the first wave of immigrants arrived in the 1830s. Most of them came seeking land, freedom, and a new start. They established their own "towns" within St. Louis: Bremen established by the Mallinckrodt family, Hyde Park, Bissell's Point, even Ballwin and the ambiguous boundaries that created Dutchtown on the south side of the city. Their religion, too, Lutheran—eventually establishing the Missouri Synod of the Lutheran Church and Concordia Seminary—was a strong evangelical force by the 1850s.

The nineteenth century in St. Louis provided a friendly environment where German was still spoken and the culture could be maintained. And well into the twentieth century, the German community was a cohesive group accounting for more than half the population and students in the public schools.

Turnvereins, combining gymnastics, physical education, and community centers throughout the city, were a concrete manifestation of German influence. Eventually the influence of the "Turners" put physical education into the public schools.

So unified and large was the German population and so catalyzed by their strong work ethic, they were successful in electing their own mayoral candidate by the end of the nineteenth century. As a powerful bloc, they pushed for needed infrastructures, and got them.

The character of the Germans, their competencies, their sense of community, their inherent virtues and values were transmitted to the St. Louis culture and became identified with it. Their folklore was a welcome, integral part of their contribution, which became one with St. Louis and was the most dominant in a city of different ethnic neighborhoods.

FOLK VOCABULARY

"Dutch" as a corruption of *"deutsch"* is the most often applied folk term for the German community in St. Louis. Used as an adjective, it became a common expression for all of St. Louis:

- Dutchtown: where the Germans were most concentrated in south St. Louis City.

- To be "in dutch": to be in trouble.

- "Dutch courage": a person with false courage because of having imbibed too much alcohol.

- "Dutch agreement": one who agreed to anything because he had had too much to drink.

- "Dutch treat": each paying for his own food at a restaurant.

- When your German guest in St. Louis asks for a "quitting stick," give him a toothpick.

- "Talk like a Dutch uncle": a firm way to raise kids; speak strongly and directly.
- "Scrubby Dutch": nickname given to Germans in St. Louis for their fastidious attention to cleanliness.
- Other communities have used the "Dutch" expressions, of course, and some of them are common folk expressions. But their application to the St. Louis German community is pervasive and has been for more than one hundred years.

Other popular expressions commonly heard in St. Louis retain the original German and become folk in their understanding by all ears:

- *Kopf Hoch!* is used as encouragement to "keep your chin up."
- *Nein, ja, jawohl, achtung, fraulein,* and *kaput* are all used in the original German for emphasis, sarcasm, anger, or even courting.
- "*Blau*," used to define drunk in German has been corrupted to the expression "plowed" to indicate that someone is beyond drunk!
- Variations in syntax are common also: "make the bed up," or "go eat yourself some," or "out the light."

Folk naming in the German community is also unique and a vestige of European life. The first name given at birth was always considered a spiritual name and represented a saint. And several boys in the same family were given the same first (spiritual) name and then addressed by their second name. John George, John Peter, and John Adam, for example, are brothers, but are known as George, Peter, and Adam.

Marty Warren from St. Louis reports a variant on the German naming practice. In his family, all first sons of first sons are given the same first name and are addressed by their middle name. John Martin Warren is Marty and John Gabriel Warren is Gabe, for example.

Girls born in St. Louis German families were also often named according to the same practice: Maria Katherine, Maria Barbara, and Maria Hilda would all be sisters, but known as Katherine, Barb, or Hilda in conversation.

FOLK EXPRESSIONS/PROVERBS

Many German sayings reflect their practical approach to life, the value of a work ethic, and the importance of speaking directly. Some are even related to recognizable American expressions that beg the folk questions of origins.

- Old John will never learn. (Can't teach an old dog new tricks.)
- He's wax in her hands. (Putty in someone's hands.)
- Kissin' don't last but cookin' do. (The way to a man's heart is through his stomach.)
- Work before pleasure.
- You make your own happiness.
  (Jeder ist seines eigenen gluckes sachnmied.)
- Don't put off til tomorrow what you can do today.
- You get what you earn. (You made your bed, now lie in it.)
  (Ohne fleiss kein preis.)
- Idleness is the beginning of all sin. (Idleness is the devil's workshop.)
- Working brings blessing.
  (Sich regen, bringt segen.)
- He who doesn't value the penny doesn't deserve the dollar. (A penny saved is a penny earned.)
- As the cap is put on, it must be worn. (You made your bed, now lie in it.)
- If you have to do it, you might as well do it right.
- Save for a rainy day.
  (Spare in der zeit, so hast du in der not.)
- Honesty is best.
- A blind hawk will even find an acorn. (Even a blind pig will find an acorn.)
- All good things come in threes. (Third time's a charm.)
- Bad luck seldom comes alone. (Bad luck usually occurs in threes.)
- She doesn't have all her cups in the cupboard. (She is not the sharpest knife in the drawer.)

SUPERSTITIONS

- If a stork builds its nest in your chimney, you will live a very long life and be wealthy. (The Bevo Mill in St. Louis, a very famous, established German restaurant, has an iconic stork in its chimney, placed there by the original owners to fulfill this belief.)

- It is not good to kill spiders. They are good luck.

- On Easter Monday, it is important to bathe in cold water, the Easter water, to have good health all year long.

- If someone whom you consider your enemy comes to your door to visit, remove some part of the dirt or grass or sod on which he/she walked and hang it on the outside of the house. When the dirt wastes away, so will the enemy.

- On St. Martin's Day, November 11, listen to which direction dogs are barking. Your marriage partner will come from that direction.

- It is believed that all animals talk on Christmas Eve to welcome the Christ Child. So an unmarried virgin must go to the barn or chicken coop at midnight and knock. The first sound she hears will determine her marriage chances in the New Year. If a hen cackles first, she will not be married; if a rooster crows, she will be married. If a cow, horse, or sheep make a noise first, she will have to wait another year to discover her marriage fate.

- At the wedding reception, when the cake is cut, small pieces of it must be threaded through the wedding ring of the bride because the cake is made up of sugar and salt—the pleasure and pain of the marriage. This means that the couple recognizes that the marriage will endure both well.

- If a pregnant woman walks over a grave in a cemetery, the child will die.

- When your child cuts his first tooth, the mother must slap his face to ensure that teething will be easier and that all teeth will come in straight.

- If a person dies in the home, all their clothes must be washed before he is buried to ensure that they can rest easily.

- Never mend clothes while someone is wearing them. It will bring bad luck to the seamstress and the wearer.

CUSTOMS

Many of Germanic descent wear their wedding rings on their right hands. The bride and groom must have matching bands and no jewels of any kind in the rings.

Richfes, the custom of "topping out," is a strong tradition in St. Louis construction. As soon as the shell of the building is complete, it is decorated with a fir tree placed on the top. This is to ensure that the building will stand forever and the people living or working in it will always have good luck and good health.

ST. MARTIN'S DAY & OKTOBERFEST

St. Martin's Feast Day on November 11 is a very important day to the German people in St. Louis. St. Martin became a monk and was a very good, righteous person who loved to work among the faithful. He was appointed Bishop of Tours because of his piety and charisma, but the appointment was against his will.

Legend tells us that St. Martin hid in the barns and coops of geese because he did not want to be a bishop. These geese, with their loud noise, betrayed Martin as he was hiding and he had to become the bishop.

Eventually fire or light festivities came to be celebrated at this time of year, the beginning of winter. St. Martin lanterns and torches are sometimes carried in a procession or lit in a church to remind everyone of the "light" of goodness and generosity that Martin symbolized. At this same time, geese are butchered—not surprising since they ratted on him—but primarily because they are ready for harvesting. The goose feathers were used for pillows and beds, eggs and fat for baking, and the feathers for dusting. But most importantly to American culture, the feathers were used to create feather Christmas trees because the Germans felt that American trees were not strong enough to hold lit candles. The feather tree has become a decorator item and an expensive purchase throughout St. Louis.

Oktoberfest, a celebration of the harvest and a preparation for the cold days of winter, has become a citywide celebration in St. Louis. German influence has reached all across the region, even into previously "pure" ethnic communities, and has transferred the meaning of the harvest to others. German beer of all varieties, bratwurst, sauerkraut, knockwurst, schnitzel, knodel, Black Forest cake or German chocolate cake, even hasenpfeffer are all served in a remembrance of the nineteenth-century Munich celebrations. Except in the St. Louis area, everyone celebrates. Even the supermarkets prepare Oktoberfest displays to give everyone an excuse to celebrate before the harshness of winter. German influence on St. Louis has become part of St. Louis culture, custom, and lore.

THE FLEA MARKET AND THE GARAGE/YARD SALE

Consistent with their cultural identity of frugality and practicality, informants of Germanic descent in St. Louis proudly claim credit for the popularity of the flea market, especially those gigantic ones held on Saturdays and for the popularity of the garage sales on the "folk" day of Wednesday and eventually, Saturday. The materials that you have accumulated can be sold at any price or what the seller accepts. And it is congruent with their folk philosophy of waste not, want not, saving a penny, and appreciating the dollar.

In St. Louis, as in other parts of the country, these sales have blossomed into "whole block sales," even subdivision sales as a folk custom of the Germanic influence in the area.

FOLK FOODS

In addition to the folk foods of Oktoberfest, which can be served all through the year, there are certain foods associated with holidays in the German community.

Stollen: Sometimes called a "fruit cake" and shaped like a flattened log with a ridge in the center, is associated in legend with the Christ Child in swaddling clothes. The "wrapping" of the stolen around fruit or other filling symbolizes Baby Jesus and is carefully and specially made at Christmas.

"*Kassler*" with sauerkraut—pork chops with sauerkraut—is made especially on New Year's Day so that whoever partakes will be rich throughout the new year and never want for money. Again, pork is used here because of superstition. The pig roots forward for his food and does not go backward, and many want to improve with their resolutions in the new year and go forward also.

On Christmas Eve, some St. Louisans of German ethnicity continue to eat fish in many different varieties. December 24 used to be a fast day for them, and they continue to observe it.

On Christmas Day, dinner is *spaetzle* (dumplings), liver dumpling soup, pork roast, Wiener schnitzel, red or white cabbage, and always potatoes. If a fresh pig could be butchered, the Christmas dinner would be a special celebration.

The pretzel, or *brezel*, although eaten at any time of the year, is associated with the holy day of Christmas. Legend tells us that its form with the arms of the pretzel crossed represents a Christian in prayer of thanksgiving for the coming of the Baby Jesus.

Whether regarding holiday food or not, the German community, with their perennially practical, no-waste mentality, always applied an important proverb: Take all you want, but eat all you take!

An interesting note on a folk food American tradition: Generally, Americans are served a glass of ice cold water with their meals, in fact, immediately as they are seated in a restaurant. Germans, particularly in St. Louis, resist the cold water with a meal because they believe it cools the stomach too much and inhibits digestion. This is one folk food custom that has not been adopted by the rest of the community.

THE LEGEND OF THE CHRISTMAS SPIDER

Historically and academically, Germany is filled with legends and lore. All of them, like the combined versions related to Santa Claus, have made their way into American Germanic lore in one form or another. But they are not exclusively the regional lore of any German community within the country. All understand them and practice some part of them, depending on the town or city culture.

The legend of the spider, however, has become extremely popular within the German community in St. Louis. The popularity of the legend, as with other lore of German origin, has crossed folk group boundaries and become a charming addition to Christmas lore and Christmas decorations.

German women are notorious for their fastidious cleaning. This is never more evident than at Christmas, when the whole household prepares for the arrival of the Baby Jesus. Days are full of work: cooking, cleaning, sewing, wrapping—all must be done to be certain that the household is ready for His arrival.

Every corner of the house, from ceiling to floor, is cleansed of any dirt. The surfaces are immaculate. But the spider, as one of God's creatures, continues to spin his webs as his nature requires. Often they produce these webs right after the housekeeper has finished her cleaning.

But because Germans believe that killing a spider will bring bad luck, they can not bring themselves to take this drastic action. They also believe that spiders, as creatures of God, were allowed to welcome Jesus and celebrate the same as the inhabitants of the household.

It happened one day that the German housekeeper saw a spider and immediately, as if in divine inspiration, thought to put the spider in the Christmas tree, nesting in the middle above the crib, where he could have a perfect view of the Child's birth. What she didn't remember was that the spider would continue to weave his web, as spiders do, and on Christmas Eve she noticed the beginning of the web throughout the middle of the tree. But she had no time to clean it out, so, against her nature, she left it in the tree.

On Christmas morning, when the whole family gathered to welcome the Baby Jesus, they noticed that the web of the spider had changed to a beautiful silvery substance that lay across the whole tree, giving it sheen and a sparkle such as they had never seen. The spider was welcoming the Baby Jesus in his own way. He created the tinsel that adorns Christmas trees all over the world. It was his special gift to the Christ Child, and has been ever since.

Industrial, saving, practical, civic minded, value driven, fun loving, heritage proud—German immigrants to St. Louis are all of these things, and their principle-centered living is strongly reflected in the lifestyle of their folklore. The solidarity of their traditions has been so influential that a whole region has adopted many of their traits. In their own words, they are the *über* folklorists of St. Louis, the *meister* of oral transmissions, and the educators of the informal learning process.

CHAPTER 12

GRAFFITI

WALL SCRAWLS AND INTERNET RAMBLINGS:
WHO SLEEPS WITH A NIGHT LIGHT?
WHO SOARS WITH TURKEYS?

IT'S AS OLD AS MAN. IT WAS FOUND IN THE PREHISTORIC CAVES OF FRANCE. It was the primary communication tool in Pompeii. It marks territory for gangs. It's a subject of civic outrage. Its commission sends people to jail. It is the subject of study in many college classrooms. And it is often the only voice of the people.

Graffiti, from the Latin *graffito*, meaning a scratch or scribbling on a wall, now appears on buttons, bumper stickers, and T-shirts. Why all this writing on walls? Answers are as varied as the anthropologists, sociologists, and psychologists who try to explain it. It may be the Freudian concept of humor, which states that it is the only mature way to offset a problem. It may be communication or even the "primal scream" in a fixed form. It could even be the only form of protest the "common man" has in a democracy where he feels that his is a voice in the wilderness. Leaving an anonymous comment on a bathroom wall—the toilet, which "everyman" must use, is a common and base denominator—allows the folk to express an emotion, an idea, a protest, an opinion that somebody will "hear" or be forced to listen to.

Notwithstanding the unsightliness of the permanent scrawl, or the obvious charge of destruction of property, the history of graffiti displays a need, whatever that might be, for this form of expression. Whole cities, worldwide, have addressed the issue, even going so far as to put up "graffiti walls" in downtown areas where people are allowed to write at will. This, theoretically, will prevent the folk from scrawling on walls all over the city. Weekly, and sometimes daily, the walls are cleaned to allow for more graffiti.

But as expected, this has not stopped "wall expressions" from appearing in more common locations, where anonymity is assured.

In this traditional approach, with different versions, anonymous authorship, and the need of the folk group for expression, graffiti will serve a purpose, the mission of which will be debated for many more years. But whatever one's opinion of it, graffiti is folklore. It will always be used by people to express their explanation of society.

Because of mass communication today, graffiti in St. Louis is often the same as that found in other locations. Subject matter relates to the political climate, the religious atmosphere, or the state of American institutions, including the family, and even personal messages of love or requests for sexual favors. It is the specific material related to the St. Louis region that helps to define the culture of the region and gives way to the grassroots opinions of the populace.

There is also an Internet phenomenon currently overwhelming the e-mail in-boxes of countless people. It's a form of graffiti, with origins often in corporate or institutional life, or expressions in a prescribed form related to concerns of the day and circulated daily to thousands and thousands of Internet users. Its purpose is humor, irony, sarcasm, or simply anger about the inordinate attention given to topics that are not important in the clichéd scheme of things. Or they might be "memo comments" on "sacred" professions such as medicine or government.

A curious aspect of these Internet graffiti-like mailings is that the same materials circulated via corporate inter-office memos as far back as the 1950s and are now surfacing on the Internet as new lore! Again, the folk concerns have not really changed in more than five decades and the need for expressing one's "voice" is still there. But with the Internet the expression can be communicated more quickly and still anonymously. No one knows where the "memo" started, but it can be sent several times a day to the same person from different friends in any part of the world. This phenomenon is not exclusively St. Louis lore, of course, but its staggering repetition makes it acceptable, and representative of St. Louisans' folk concerns and explanations.

GRAFFITI

Do not write on the walls
(Different handwriting underneath)
You want me to type?
>   (Found in Famous-Barr department store bathroom)

The gene pool in St. Louis could use a little chlorine.

Look at our government; George Orwell was an optimist.

Yesterday is but a memory.
(Different writing underneath)
Tomorrow but a vision.
(Different writing underneath)
Today is a bitch!
>   (Tavern in south St. Louis City)

Start the day off with a smile and get it over with.

Give your child mental blocks for Christmas.

Did you know that Sara Lee was a diabetic?

I give up; nobody cares about me.
(Different writing underneath)
You're right—give up; who cares?
(Different writing underneath)
My God cares; I talked to him this morning.
(Different writing underneath)
Sweetheart, we care at Schnucks!
>   (Found in a National Food Store no longer in St. Louis; Schnucks is the largest grocery chain in the St. Louis area.)

Change is inevitable except from a vending machine.

If you are psychic, think HONK!

St. Louis radiator—a great place to take a leak.

Disarm all rapists.
(Different writing underneath)
It's not their arms I'm worried about.
  (Found in a Famous-Barr restroom)

My mother made me a homosexual.
(Different writing underneath)
If I give her the wool, will she make me one?

God is coming to St. Louis—tickets on sale now.

God is not dead. He just couldn't find a parking place in Clayton.

St. Louis is not dead. It just seems so because it's next to exciting
  Arnold.

You don't buy Budweiser here. You just rent it.
  (In a tavern in St. Louis county)

Down with graffiti.
(Different handwriting underneath)
Yeah, down with all Italians!

(An arrow pointing to the toilet paper; found at Washington
  University in St. Louis)
Course syllabus, take one.

Mayor Slay sleeps with a night light
(Or Cervantes, Tucker, or Conway—these former St. Louis mayors
  also have been named in graffiti.)

Don't be a high school dropout.
(Written underneath on the poster.)
No, stay in the St. Louis Public Schools and learn to read and riot!

St. Louis is alive and living in Kansas City.

The world is flat. Signed Class of 1491
(Underneath in different handwriting)
All the girls in my class are flat. Signed Class of 1987

Veni, vidi, wiwi.
(On men's room in a St. Louis City saloon.)

You can't win except through ignorance. Look at the Public Schools.

Keep St. Louis green. Throw your trash in East St. Louis.

Support St. Louis's finest. Bribe a cop today.

I want to seduce my history teacher.
(Different handwriting underneath)
I did and got an F.

Of course, I smoke in St. Louis. It's safer than breathing.

Little Jack Horner has more serious problems than he thinks.

Graffiti is now respectable. Just read the Post-Dispatch.

Bush was the first president to have a Dick for a vice president.
(Different writing underneath)
No, Eisenhower was.

A St. Louis criminal lawyer is a redundancy.

Missouri Lottery: a tax on people who are bad at math.

No one listens to me until I fart.

Express Lane: Five beers or less.
(Sign over a urinal in a St. Louis tavern)

Make love, not war.
(Different writing underneath)
Do both—get married!

Remember, beauty is only a light switch away.

All stressed out and no one to choke.

And your point is?

God made us sisters, Prozac made us friends.

The ocean would be deeper without sponges.

Kids in the back seat cause accidents.
(Different writing underneath)
Accidents in the back seat cause kids.

Tell the truth, you won't have to remember anything.

Free love costs too much.

A friend in need is useless.

INTERNET GRAFFITI

Baby Boomers—no surprise—have contributed more folklore through the computer than any other group. As a generation they have been responsible for the enormous impact of the computer. And living longer than any other demographic, the aging process gives them an opportunity to reflect on their lives. It may not always be a pleasant reflection, but it allows for perspective, commonality, and definition. The romance of nostalgia helps as a coping mechanism, and the computer becomes the quick transmitter of this lore to Boomers everywhere.

REMEMBER WHEN?

- Decisions were made by going "eenie-meenie-minie-mo."
- Mistakes were corrected by simply exclaiming, "do over!"
- "Race issue" meant arguing about who ran the fastest.
- Money issues were handled by whoever was the banker in Monopoly.
- Catching fireflies happily occupied an entire evening.
- It wasn't odd to have two or three best friends.
- Being old referred to anyone over twenty.
- The net on a tennis court was the perfect height to play volleyball and rules didn't matter.
- The worst thing you could catch from the opposite sex was cooties.
- It was magic when you father would "remove" his thumb.

- Having a weapon in school meant you were caught with a slingshot.
- Nobody was prettier than Mom, and Dad was the strongest man alive.
- Scrapes were kissed and became instantly better.
- Abilities were discovered because of a "double dare."
- Saturday morning cartoons were not thirty-minute commercials for action figures.
- "Olly-Olly-Oxen free" made perfect sense.
- War was a card game.
- Baseball cards laced through the spokes made any bike a motorcycle.
- Water balloons were the ultimate weapon.
- Ice cream was a basic food group.

And another nostalgic, but humorous, look at growing old to Boomers covers all aspects of life.

THE BENEFITS OF GETTING OLDER

1. Kidnappers are not very interested in you.

2. In a hostage situation you are likely to be released first.

3. It's harder and harder for sexual harassment charges to stick.

4. No one expects you to run into a burning building.

5. People call at 9 p.m. and ask, "Did I wake you?"

6. People no longer view you as a hypochondriac.

7. There's nothing left to learn the hard way.

8. Things you buy now won't wear out.

9. You can eat dinner at 4 p.m.

10. You can live without sex but not without glasses.

11. You enjoy hearing about other people's operations.

12. You get into a heated argument about pension plans.

13. You have a party and the neighbors don't even realize it.

14. You no longer think of speed limits as a challenge.

15. You sing along to elevator music.

16. Your eyes won't get much worse.

17. Your joints are more accurate than the National Weather Service.

18. Your secrets are safe with your friends because they can't remember them either.

19. Your supply of brain cells is finally down to a manageable size.

Of course, all the Baby Boomers are undergoing medical "tests" to prevent, find, or predict some problem area. They are bombarded from all sides about the importance of preventive health. The colonoscopy, both feared and embarrassing, has become a favorite topic of conversation. Folk humor helps the acceptance. After all, Boomers reflect, "At our age, why not laugh at it?"

COMMENTS MADE BY PATIENTS UNDERGOING A COLONOSCOPY

- Take it easy, doc. You're boldly going where no man has gone before.

- Find Amelia Earhart yet?

- Can you hear me NOW?

- Are we there yet? Are we there yet? Are we there yet?

- You know, in Arkansas, we're legally married now.

- Any sign of the trapped miners, chief?

- You put your left hand in; you take your left hand out. You do the Hokey Pokey . . .

- Hey, now I know how the Muppets feel.

- If your hand doesn't fit, you must acquit.

- Hey, Doc, let me know if you find my dignity.
- You used to be an executive at Enron didn't you?
- Could you write me a note for my wife, saying that my head is not, in fact, up there?

Corporate life, with its mysterious infrastructure and distributed wealth, has not escaped Internet graffiti either. Since the folk within the rank and file cannot control the decision-making, they need to explain it to themselves. Again, the humor of folklore helps in the understanding.

For example, the annual performance appraisal is an established practice for most corporations. Often promotions, raises, and even improvement plans are based on "what the boss writes."

The following, computer folklore tells us, were taken from actual appraisals:

- This employee is depriving a village somewhere of an idiot.
- This young lady has delusions of adequacy.
- I would not allow this employee to breed.
- His people would follow him anywhere but only out of morbid curiosity.
- He sets low personal standards and then consistently fails to achieve them.
- Works well only under constant supervision and when cornered like a rat.

And here's some advice.

TEN BEST THINGS TO SAY TO THE BOSS WHEN YOU ARE CAUGHT SLEEPING AT YOUR DESK

1. "They told me at the blood bank that this might happen."
2. "This is just a fifteen-minute power nap like they raved about in the 'Time Management' course you sent me to."

3. "Whew! Guess I left the top off the white-out. You probably got here just in time."

4. "I wasn't sleeping. I was meditating on the mission statement and envisioning a new paradigm." (All buzzwords in corporate America.)

5. "I was testing my keyboard for drool resistance."

6. "I was doing a highly specific yoga exercise to relieve work-related stress. Do you discriminate against people who practice yoga?"

7. "Why did you interrupt me? I had almost figured out a solution to our biggest problem."

8. "The coffee machine is broken."

9. "Someone must have put decaf in the wrong pot."

10. ". . . in Jesus' name, Amen."

Education, religion, insurance, medicine—sacred institutions—are the object of computer lore with written malaprops. Students' answers to questions, doctors' notes on patients' charts, insurance documents, and even church bulletins have all been accused of using inappropriate modifiers and not noticing the effect. This also was collected as lore from the 1950s through the 1990s and circulated orally, but the computer has become the transmitter, and the verbal gaffes are sent and re-sent on monthly bases. In the vein of urban belief tales, they are documented as having "actually happened." Whether they did or not, they represent our skepticism to the institutions involved in the lore.

COLLECTED FROM ST. LOUIS STUDENTS' ANSWERS TO VARIOUS QUESTIONS ON TESTS

- Germinate: to become a naturalized German.
- Vacuum: A large, empty space where the Pope lives.
- Dew is formed on leaves when the sun shines down on them and makes them perspire.
- A fossil is an extinct animal. The older it is, the more extinct it is.
- Blood flows down one leg and up the other.

- Sir Francis Drake circumcised the world in a 100-foot clipper.

- Rural life is lived mostly in the country.

- To be a good nurse, you must be absolutely sterile.

- Running is a unique experience and I thank God for exposing me to the track team.

- To keep milk from turning sour, keep it in the cow.

- To remove dust from the eye, pull the eye down over the nose.

- For a nosebleed: put the nose much lower than the body until the heart stops.

- For a head cold, use an agonizer (sic) to spray the nose until it drops into your throat.

- For fainting, rub a person's chest. If it's a lady, rub her arm.

- For fainting, put the head between the knees of the nearest doctor.

FINISH THE PROVERB: A THIRD GRADE CLASS IN ST. LOUIS ANSWERED THE FOLLOWING

- Better to be safe than . . . punch a sixth grader.

- Don't bite the hand that . . . looks dirty.

- You can't teach an old dog new . . . math.

- The pen is mightier than the . . . pigs.

- A penny saved is . . . not much.

- If you lie down with dogs, you'll . . . stink in the morning.

- If at first you don't succeed . . . get new batteries.

- You get out of something what you . . . see pictured on the box.

- You can lead a horse to water but . . . how?

TAKEN FROM ST. LOUIS CHURCH BULLETINS

- Irving Benson and Jessie Carter were married on October 24 in the church. So ends a friendship that began in school days.

- The ladies of the church have cast off clothing of every kind, and they can be seen in the church basement Friday afternoon.

- The service will close with "Little Drops of Water." One of the men will start quietly and the rest of the congregation will join in.

- This being Easter Sunday, we will ask Mrs. White to come forward to lay an egg on the altar.

- This afternoon there will be meetings in the north and south ends of the church. Children will be baptized on both ends.

- Wednesday, the Ladies Literary Society will meet. Mrs. Johnson will sing "Put Me in My Little Bed," accompanied by the Reverend.

- Thursday at 8 p.m., there will be a meeting of the Little Mothers' Club. All those wishing to become Little Mothers, please meet the minister in his study.

- On Sunday, a special collection will be taken to defray the expense of the new carpet. All those wishing to do something on the carpet, please come forward and get a piece of paper.

A ST. LOUIS INSURANCE COMPANY COLLECTED THESE EXPLANATIONS FOR ACCIDENTS

- Coming home I drove into the wrong house and collided with a tree I don't have.

- I collided with a stationary truck coming the other way.

- A truck backed through my windshield into my wife's face.

- A pedestrian hit me and went under my car.

- The guy was all over the road. I had to swerve a number of times before I hit him.

- I pulled away from the side of the road, glanced at my mother-in-law, and headed towards the embankment.

- I had been driving my car for forty years when I fell asleep at the wheel and had an accident.

- I told the police that I was not injured, but on removing my hat, I found that I had a skull fracture.

- I saw this slow-moving, sad-faced old gentleman as he bounced off the hood of my car.

- The telephone pole was approaching fast. I was attempting to swerve out of its path when it struck my front end.

- To avoid hitting the bumper of the car in front, I struck the pedestrian.
- I was on the way to the doctor with rear end trouble when my universal joint gave way, causing me to have an accident.

All these mis-modifiers are laughable and certainly possible, but perhaps they are funny because they poke fun at the sacredness and the purposeful complexity of the insurance industry.

Doctors and hospitals and all their procedures are the proverbial Greek to most people. So an investigation of what doctors and/or nurses have written on patients' charts or recorded as notes reveal "humanness" that is delightful to the folk themselves.

MEDICAL FOLKLORE: SAID TO HAVE BEEN WRITTEN ON PATIENTS' CHARTS

- The patient has chest pain if she lies on her left side for over a year.
- On the second day the knee was better and on the third day it disappeared completely.
- The patient has been depressed ever since she has been seeing me in 1983.
- The patient is tearful and crying constantly. She also appears to be depressed.
- Discharge status: Alive but without permission.
- The patient refused an autopsy.
- Healthy appearing decrepit 69-year-old male, mentally alert but forgetful.
- Between you and me we ought to be able to get this woman pregnant.
- She is numb from her toes down.
- Since she can't get pregnant with her husband, I thought you might like to work her up.
- The skin was moist and dry.

- Rectal exam revealed a normal size thyroid.

- She stated that she had been constipated for most of her adult life until she got a divorce.

- Exam of genitalia reveals that he is circus-sized (sic).

- The lab test indicated abnormal lover function.

- Skin: somewhat pale but present.

- Patient was seen by Dr. White who felt we should sit on the abdomen and I agree.

- On examination, when he pulled his pants down, I was surprised to see his beeper dangling there.

- She wakes up every morning with a new pain in the neck.

- When she fainted, her eyes rolled around the room.

Understanding the sexes has been one of those "time forever" formal studies and paradoxes that all classes of folk groups have been discussing for hundreds of years. Again, the computer can dispense opinions quickly and to a very large audience to keep the argument alive.

COMPUTER LORE ON UNDERSTANDING THE SEXES
HOW TO IMPRESS A WOMAN

- Compliment her
- Respect her
- Honor her
- Cuddle her
- Kiss her
- Caress her
- Love her
- Stroke her
- Tease her
- Comfort her

- Protect her
- Hug her
- Hold her
- Wine and dine her
- Spend money on her
- Listen to her
- Stand by her
- Hold her
- Go to the ends of the earth for her

HOW TO IMPRESS A MAN

- Show up naked
- Bring food

Written by a man or a woman? Who knows? It's transmitted everywhere, anonymously, and expresses a current belief on relationships. And as with other Internet lore, it is disseminated more quickly than the traditional lore.

A more popular discussion on the communication skills of the sexes is a throwback from the 1970s when linguists were first publishing their results for a mass audience. The Internet has picked up on the argument, and it has grown as graffiti on a wall. Readers add their own definition, making the folk involvement complete. Consider how we communicate in folk style:

WHAT IT REALLY MEANS

- "I can't find it." REALLY MEANS
  "It didn't fall into my outstretched hands, so I am completely clueless."
- "That's women's work." REALLY MEANS
  "It's dirty, difficult and thankless."
- "Will you marry me?" REALLY MEANS

"Both my roommates have moved out. I can't find the washer, and there is no more peanut butter."

- "It's a guy thing." REALLY MEANS
  "There is no rational thought pattern connected with it, and you have no chance at all of making it logical."

- "Can I help with the dinner?" REALLY MEANS
  "Why isn't it already on the table?"

- "It would take too long to explain." REALLY MEANS
  "I have no idea how it works."

- "I'm getting more exercise lately." REALLY MEANS
  "The batteries in the remote are dead."

- "We're going to be late." REALLY MEANS
  "Now I have a legitimate excuse to drive like a maniac."

- "Take a break, honey, you're working too hard." REALLY MEANS
  "I can't hear the game over the vacuum cleaner."

- "That's interesting, dear." REALLY MEANS
  "Are you still talking?"

- "Honey, we don't need material things to prove our love."
  REALLY MEANS
  "I forgot our anniversary."

- "You know how bad my memory is." REALLY MEANS
  "I remember the words to the theme song of 'F Troop,' the address of the first girl I kissed, the vehicle identification number of every car I've ever owned, but I forgot your birthday."

- "I do help around the house." REALLY MEANS
  "I once threw a dirty towel near the laundry basket."

As in all scrawls on the wall, sentiments can be added as they are considered—except the computer does it quicker, with more readers and more correspondents. The scenarios are endless, and the male-female discussion continues.

Another way in which paperwork folklore has taken hold is in the "real-but-phony-official-letter-practical-joke," which mirrors the official commerce of institutions but is not really "official." Actual letterhead from an establishment is used to inform someone of something dire or

STATE OF MISSOURI

DEPARTMENT OF MENTAL HEALTH

MALCOM BLISS MENTAL HEALTH CENTER

1420 Grattan Street
St. Louis, Missouri 63104

Thomas H. Smith, M.D.
Superintendent

Larry C. McLevy
Assistant Superintendent
Administration

OPHTHAMOLOGY DEPT.

Dear _____

    Please be advised that your Optrectomy operation is scheduled
for _____*April 1, 1981*_____ . The purpose of this delicate operation
is to sever the cord that connects your eyes to your rectum and hopefully
get rid of your shitty outlook on life.

Sincerely yours,

Thomas H. Smith, M.D.
Robert Lindsey, Surgical Assistant

---

of the results of a "phony" medical procedure or something intimidating. Often a folk slang expression is used in the narrative of the letter, and that helps the reader to "get the joke." But the initial reading, by the very nature of the official envelope and letterhead, is stressful and is meant to be.

The following example has made the rounds in St. Louis for more than a decade. Origins were never discovered. But Malcolm Bliss was a famous hospital in the St. Louis region that treated people with psychological problems. Its very name was often used in slang expressions or folk sayings. "She's a candidate for Malcolm Bliss," for example, when the speaker had never even been to the place. Even though Malcolm Bliss has closed its doors, the identification of some psychological disorder with its name continues to be used by the folk in St. Louis. It's understandable to identify the stress of someone who receives a letter from the place with the official envelope and letterhead announcing some news.

It would not be a stretch to look for underlying reasons for the proliferation of folklore on the Internet created by the unprecedented rise of stress in American society. We are being told constantly that daily stressors are exponentially greater than they were sixty, fifty, ten, or even five years ago. The speed of the information age, the body of knowledge heaved at us daily; the demands on our time from unlikely sources have all of us demanding a balance between work and life, family and work, or quiet time and the rat race. Much of this discussion on stress is reduced to a joke, an anecdote, or even a silly plea intended to diffuse the predicted dire consequences of a stressful life.

One of the more popular folk expressions of what the folk would secretly like to do for stress management is related in the following example. There are different versions of the "reduction," but they all have the same intent, i.e., "I can't take it anymore." But the therapy is in the writing and sending of the message, not the actual action.

STRESS REDUCTION

- Take two minutes to reduce stress and be more productive.
- Picture yourself near a stream.
- Birds are softly chirping in the crisp, cool, mountain air.
- Nothing can bother you here. No one knows this secret place.
- You are in total seclusion from that place called "the world."
- The soothing sound of a gentle waterfall fills the air with a cascade of serenity.
- The water is clear.

- You can easily make out the face of the person whose head you're holding under the water.

- Look! It's the person who caused all this stress in the first place.

- What a pleasant surprise!

- You let him go . . . just for a quick breath . . . then plop! . . . back under he goes.

- You allow yourself as many deep breaths as you want.

There now . . . feeling better?????

So folklore continues to be transmitted in the quickest of ways, identifying the issues of importance to the folk group, ironically, and often sarcastically, giving their opinion of the situation, and understanding that there is nothing they can do about it. But the function of folklore as compensation or validation operates very well in this computer lore. The complexity of the society is beyond our ken, but we can still use it to let the world know that the folk have their opinions. Electronic graffiti lives!

So, if your grandmother asks you to send her a .jpeg file of your newborn so she can create a new screen saver, or if you just tried to enter your password on the microwave, you understand!

CHAPTER 13

A CASE STUDY OF A ST. LOUIS FAMILY

Rosemary Wickes Intagliata, a native St. Louisan and a seventy-eight-year-old dynamo reminiscent of Auntie Mame, is a living, breathing, proud, walking advertisement for the critical importance of lore in a family culture. Her very life, within her extended family, is a *paean* to the value of diversity and the many positive, life-affirming results of maintaining the vital folk concept of learning and growing from each other.

Rosemary, with the folk nickname of Poad, was born in St. Louis among the "scrubby Dutch" and has lived in the larger community all her life. She was the youngest of three children of Norine and George Wickes. Baptized a Catholic, raised a Catholic, still a practicing "practical" Catholic, she married Russell Intagliata and produced four children: Elizabeth ("Little Betty" to distinguish her from her aunt Betty), Christine, Ed, and Marie (Mimi).

The marriage created a new lore for Rosemary in an informal education with the Italian culture by which she tempered her own family lore. Her husband, Russ, was one of eleven children, and the extended family became the stereotypical robust, boisterous, loving, fun, and demonstrative Italian "mob" in the very best of senses.

So in the world of her German upbringing, fused with the mores of the Italians and touched by the experience of living in America, Rosemary enthusiastically embraced the lore of her new culture, but remembering her roots, created and adapted a strong, personal lore from the diversity of her connections.

Thirty-five years into her marriage, Rosemary became a divorce statistic and had to endure an unwelcome rite of passage. This was not without its trauma and personal recriminations, but the survivor in her took over and reasserted itself in short order. A new role with its own lore was added to her growing social style. Being a "divorcee" did not become the stigma it had been to her generation but instead became for her the encouragement to learn from life's lessons and to "get on with it" with considerable potential and optimism.

During this "necessary loss" of her adult life, Rosemary's children were developing their own lifestyles different from the foundational lore of the Wickes-Intagliata culture. Betty, a teacher by profession, divorced and then remarried. Christine married a man of the Jewish faith, and she not only converted but kept her maiden name and has adopted two children. Ed married a woman who already had two grown children. And Mimi declared she was gay, had a commitment service with her partner, and produced two children through artificial insemination.

Within this core family of Rosemary's, the very pattern of diversity acceptance is ideally present. Each of the members has an identity he or she maintains, but their commitment to the core family, the informal learning process they acquired, the lessons from the "dining room table," and even the nonjudgmental acceptance have all combined to make a strong, bonded family tied together with respect and sprinkled with the effective traditions of the family lore.

For decades Rosemary has volunteered at a children's hospital in St. Louis on a weekly basis—sometimes more frequently—doing what she has to do. She also volunteers at an agency in St. Louis that cares for babies stricken with AIDS. This has also been a labor of love for her for many years. It is just something that she "has to do." Her upbringing dictates this volunteerism, not just to sewing circle or church bazaar activities, but to places where there is a real need, giving no heed to race, ethnicity, or gender.

She also finds time to be a companion to a daughter-in-law who has a debilitating illness and lives out of town. On a regular basis, she visits her daughter and her partner and their two kids and takes part in their customs. Importantly, she also makes certain that her Jewish daughter and her family are able to celebrate their holidays along with those of her other kids. There is a real opportunity to learn from each other, she believes, and to deepen their respect for each other, not to mention the family bond.

All of this—yes, all of this—that Rosemary accomplishes, revolves around family lore: the traditions, the rituals, the food, the expressions, the aphorisms, the superstitions, the holidays, the raising of kids, the vocabulary, the folk songs, the games. And they are remembered, discussed, practiced, and applied. They are the family mortar.

In a real sense, Rosemary serves as a matriarch not only for her core family but also for her extended family. Having buried a mother, a father, a sister, a brother, and even a nephew, she serves as the protector, the advice giver, the philosopher for the children of her siblings. She talks to them regularly over the phone, invites them to the "family things," and is an integral part of their lives. Even her Italian extended family is part of her celebrations. Her connections, through the importance of family, cannot be exaggerated and can primarily be tied to her need to maintain the "family threads," which are culturally becoming thinner and thinner. Her survivor instincts require no less.

So here is Rosemary: mother, wife, grandmother, mother-in-law, great-grandmother, grandmother by marriage, volunteer, cantor, cousin, divorcee, sister-in-law, daughter-in-law, great aunt, and a survivor who loves every day of her life and would not change any of it—but all connected and underscored by her role as keeper of the lore. She is the modern version of a *griot* in the most basic of institutions.

The fieldwork among the Wickes/Intagliata family, which follows, is a combination of participant observation, interviews, and documented family history. Elizabeth (Betty) Intagliata Warren understands the academic applications and functions of folklore. The texts that follow are a combination of her research and the methodology of the folklorist.

FOLK VOCABULARY AND PROVERBS

"Many of my family's speech patterns can be blamed on the fact that at least two generations were raised without ever leaving South St. Louis. There is a list of dialect features that both the Intagliata and Wickes sides of the family share:

- We pronounce all 'or' words as if they were 'ar.' 'Born' is a homonym for 'barn.' 'Corn' rhymes with 'yarn.' 'Fork' rhymes with 'park.' And 'short' rhymes with 'part.'

- We also have a tendency to knock syllables out of words. 'Mirror' became 'meer.' 'Poem' became 'pome.' Pecan was always 'puhcahn.'

- The words 'pumpkin' and 'sandwich' were regularly slaughtered into 'punkin' and 'sannwich.'

- The word 'at' was added to verbs to denote an exact spot rather than a general area, i.e., 'staying at,' 'sitting at,' 'eating at,' 'being at,' etc.

- It was always 'going down the basement,' not 'to' or 'into' the basement.

"Rosemary appeared to have dialect oddities that were all her own.

- She pronounced 'wash' as if it had an 'r' in it. Soon all of her children were using the same pronunciation.

- Rather than a simple negative or affirmative answer, she would say, 'Yeah, uh-huh, uh-huh . . .' or 'No, uh huh, uh huh.'

- She would say, 'I'd just as leave' instead of 'I'd just as soon.'

- With regularity, she said, 'I could care less,' when she meant 'I couldn't care less.'

- 'Slobberhonous' was a drooling baby.

"Grandma Norine Wickes always made a distinction between someone who 'shopped,' that is, went to a department store, and someone who 'grocery shopped.' The latter went to the grocery store to buy a week or two of groceries. One never went just plain 'shopping' if you went to a grocery store.

"My mother, Rosemary, was the all-time queen of euphemisms. Although never a prude, she just didn't want us to use the 'proper' word for some things when we were kids. She found the words distasteful.

- We were not allowed to say 'pee' or 'poop' for bathroom words but had to say 'tinkle,' 'B.M.,' or 'potty.'

- We had to say 'pass wind' or 'pass gas' instead of 'fart.' As a matter of fact, I didn't even know 'fart' was a word until I was in high school!

- The words 'snot' and 'booger' were never used, and there were no substitutes because they simply were not things you discussed.

- When something was disgusting, it was 'acksey.'

- The word 'butt' was considered too strong, so she used 'fanny' or 'goozoo.' Her sister, Betty, used the same words with her kids also.

- Unlike her parents, who frequently used ethnic slurs, she allowed none to reach her ears. We could have gotten by with 'damn' much quicker than with the slurs for "Negro" or "Italian.".

- The best curse word Rosemary could muster was 'shoot,' 'darn,' 'go to Hades,' and 'hell's bells.'

- 'Different' was always used when making a comment on something that she didn't like or did not know what to say.

"Folk naming was also a habit of my mother. Some of the names stuck with the kids and are a source of direct application, depending on the situation. We have often been called 'Jezebel,' 'Tillie,' 'Sam,' 'Pete,' 'Mathilda,' and 'Mergatroid.' When we heard these names, we came to attention.

"Proverbs were also an important part of our family's lore. And the expressions were purposeful in their applications.

- When Rosemary was confronted with anyone's ideas of revenge or one-upmanship (especially her children's), she could be counted on to say: 'Two wrongs don't make a right.'

- When one of us complained about something someone had said, our father, Russ, always said: 'Consider the source.'

- Grandpa George Wickes used metaphors all the time, very often without any connection to the situation. But they were colorful: 'Blacker than the inside of a motorman's glove,' or 'Uglier than a mud fence on a rainy day,' or 'Bigger than three ax handles and a plug of tobacco wide.'

- My mother hated to hear us, or anyone for that matter, talk badly of another person. She would shut us up with, 'If you can't say something nice about someone, don't say anything at all.'

- Like Atticus Finch in *To Kill a Mockingbird*, my father thought it was important that all of us be able to see things from another person's point of view. To achieve this, he'd answer many of our complaints with comments prefaced by 'Look at it this way,' or 'Stand in his shoes a minute,' or 'What if you were in his place,' or 'How would you feel if you were him?'

- Grandfather Wickes also influenced my mother with his proverbial comparisons. She used many of his metaphors around us: 'madder than a wet hen,' 'red as a beet,' or 'slower than molasses.' She also liked: 'So tight he squeaks.' And 'he has more money (or whatever) than Carter has liver pills.'

- Although Rosemary was never really a practitioner of corporal punishment, she often threatened with 'I'll hang you up,' or 'I'll skin you alive,' or 'I'll beat your ears in' or 'I'll slap you silly.'

- My aunt, Betty Wickes Braun, also, was a mentor of folk phrases to my mother. She'd say: 'Don't be so sassy,' or 'Mind your p's and q's,' and, especially when we thought we were hurt, 'No blood, no sympathy.'

- When kids got restless with nothing to do, my mother would always say, 'Go outside and blow the stink off.'

SUPERSTITIONS

- Grandmother Jenni Intagliata believed in the "evil eye" and had the gesture to prove it.

- We always knocked on wood whenever we said something that tempted fate.

- Grandma Norine Wickes did not like to sit at a table set for thirteen for it would bring bad luck. She also threw salt over her left shoulder whenever she spilled the salt shaker.

- We learned never to put a hat on the bed as it would bring bad luck.

- And we were never to leave a house by a different door than that which we entered. That would also bring bad luck.

- Our family practices folk medicine for common ailments. Aspirin, for instance, cured all illnesses. And a hot toddy would also cure a cold or the flu. The whiskey helped in the curing process. Kimmel, a liqueur, was used to cure stomach aches.

- At a baby or wedding shower, the giver of the first gift opened would either have the next baby or be married next.

- When playing cards: Cut 'em thin, sure to win; Cut 'em deep, sure to weep.

- Lulubelle became a superstition and a supernatural legend all in one. Aunt Juanita Intagliata wanted us to stay out of the third-floor bedroom in her house, so she told us that a mean old lady named Lulubelle lived up there and did not like children! Lulubelle became our "boogie man," and still is today!

- Whenever we wished for good luck, we always crossed our fingers, and still do.

FOLK TALES

When folklore is discussed most people think of familiar stories told around campfires. Everyone has a favorite ghost story, supernatural legend, or moralistic tale that he or she remembers. But the personal tale is the domain of the family and has special meaning and connection for years to come.

The tale is often contrived to teach a valuable lesson, but it is specifically tailored to the needs of the family at the time. However, the tale remains part of the family for generations and is often used in a similar function when the need arises. It represents a definition of an ideal family lore because it follows all the criteria of folklore and operates on an added level of family bonding.

BETTY INTAGLIATA WARREN GIVES MORE BACKGROUND AND EXAMPLES

"My parents frequently told their children stories, usually while the children ate or during car trips. Many were the usual fairy tales like 'Cinderella,' 'Snow White,' or 'Goldilocks.' Always the moral in the story line was emphasized and sometimes was deliberately chosen to deter a particular childish crime, as in 'The Boy Who Cried Wolf.'

But there were stories their children still recall that they made up themselves, although we didn't know at the time. They were intended to persuade their children to eat, especially the oldest, Betty, for whom eating was a chore the first ten years of her life.

Here are some examples:

THE GIRL WHO WOULDN'T EAT

Once upon a time (they always began with this formulaic phrase) there was a little girl who never wanted to eat her meals. No matter what her parents said or did she refused to eat. One day when she walked outside she began to feel a little funny, and before she knew it she began to float up off the ground. She started crying and calling for her parents who came running out to see what was wrong. They saw their daughter flying as high as the rooftop. They had no idea what to do, so the mother ran in and called the doctor. The doctor said to get a plate of food and the tallest ladder they could find, and begin feeding the little girl. Well, that's what the parents did. The father held the ladder while the mother climbed up and began giving the little girl spoonfuls of food. After a few bites, the little girl dropped enough to allow her mother to descend a step. Little by little, as the girl ate, she dropped closer and closer to earth. Finally, as the mother put the last bite of food into her daughter's mouth, the little girl just touched the ground. The little girl had learned her lesson for good. From that day on she always cleaned her plate.

THE LITTLE BOY WHO WOULDN'T EAT

Once upon a time there was a little boy who never wanted to eat anything but candy. When dinnertime came he would always push his plate away, and then a little while later he would go and get some candy. His parents were very upset but didn't know what to do about it. One day the little boy got some candy to eat, but when he started to chew it, he found out he couldn't. His teeth had all gotten soft and he couldn't chew anything! Crying, he ran to his mother and told her what had happened. Immediately she called the doctor to find out what to do. He told her to start with some soft, but nutritious food, so that the boy could start building up his teeth again. The mother made some mashed potatoes and the little boy ate them. Then she made some vegetables and they found that the boy's teeth were strong enough to eat them. Finally, she made some meat, and by this time, the boy's teeth were strong enough to chew the meat. Well, the little boy had certainly learned his lesson. If he wanted strong teeth from now on, he would eat all his nutritious food at his meals and only a little bit of candy.

THE STRING BEANS THAT CRIED

Once upon a time there was a little boy who ate his meals very nicely—unless his mother served string beans. His mother tried everything to get him to eat his string beans, but nothing worked. One evening she told him that he could not leave the table until he ate his string beans. Well the little boy sat there and sat there and it got later and later and later . . . seven, eight, nine o'clock. When it was two hours past the boy's bedtime, the mother gave up, scraped the string beans into the garbage can, and told the little boy to go to bed. Later the boy awoke to the sound of crying. He listened carefully and finally decided that the sound was coming from the kitchen. He got out of bed, crept to the kitchen and looked in. He couldn't see anything but the sound was coming from there. Listening more carefully he realized that the sound was coming from the garbage can, so he went to the garbage and looked in. There, to his surprise, were all his string beans from dinner sobbing loudly. "You don't like us," they cried. "I'm sorry," was all the little boy could think of to say. "We were grown to be eaten and make people strong," they said. "Now because you wouldn't eat us, we'll end up in the garbage truck."

The little boy felt very bad for the poor string beans, so he promised them that from now on he would eat his string beans so that they could do the job they were meant to do. And he kept his promise.

"These stories were frequently interrupted by reminders such as, 'Keep eating,' and 'Pick up your fork,' because the stories were so engrossing we children would often forget what we were supposed to be doing. Whichever parent was narrating would also be wielding a spoon into one or more mouths throughout the story."

FOLK GESTURES

"Coming from an Italian family it is not surprising that folk gestures were a part of our informal education. Whenever we saw the signs, we knew that no words were necessary.

"My father would tap his head with his index finger while muttering *desta duda*, meaning 'hard head.' Eventually he did not have to use the words.

"An index finger scraping an index finger always meant, 'Shame on you.' Again words were never necessary.

"Arms folded on the chest or the hands on the hips meant anger or impatience and again no words were needed.

"The Italian side of my family would loosely extend an arm, palm up, hand bouncing slightly and sometimes they would say, "Hey, whatsa matta you?" Eventually we picked up the sign language without the words!"

CUSTOMS

"Our family celebrated holidays in traditional ways when we were kids. Now that we are married and have a larger extended family, we incorporate and blend traditions from other cultures, married into our core group, and relish the enhancement, the merging, and the education.

"But when we were kids, the Christmas decoration of the tree was always traditional. On December 23 there was always a 'Family Decorating of the Tree Party,' which included my parents and any of the children who did not believe in Santa Claus anymore. The participants grew yearly, as you can imagine. When the decorating was done, my father always got Steak 'n Shake hamburgers and malts while my mother stacked the presents around the tree. She then put up blankets and sheets to hide the room from the eyes of the kids who still believed in Santa Claus. Santa was still supposed to be working in the room. Then on Christmas Eve the room was unveiled so that everyone could see Santa's work.

"But before we opened presents we always had the traditional meal of peasant soup, homemade bread, and a relish tray."

A LIFE CONNECTED

By using the traditions of a lore, and perhaps not even realizing it, the Intagliata family and extended family have cemented a bond, often invisible and undefined, but real and meaningful. Reflection upon the vocabulary, expressions, celebrations, superstitions, folk tales, or any folklore informally learned and applied creates a history—gained and defined in no other way.

In the end, when life intrudes in unforeseen ways, as it always does, the tradition of the lore sustains them. And they can remember, reminisce, recall, and continue the customs. Nothing can destroy the bonds of family folklore.

CHAPTER 14

THE POWER
OF THE ARCH
ST. LOUIS'S INTERNATIONAL FOLK LEGEND

In my first volume of *Passing It On*, I included a folk legend about the Gateway Arch, which rises above St. Louis on the banks of the Mississippi. At 630 feet, the Arch is the tallest monument in the United States and world renowned for its execution and its symbolism.

I received dozens of notes about the legend, many with variations, and many who "validated" the theme of the legend. Some folk actually believe in the power of the Arch and even document when and how often the folktale is true. Meteorologists in St. Louis, with tongue firmly planted in cheek, brag about the power they have with just one flip of the "weather clicker." One added that he never uses the clicker during high volume days as tourists may be in the Arch! He did not know how many St. Louis meteorologists own the controlling clickers, and he wanted to remain anonymous!

Here's the tale as I reported it earlier:

THE POWER OF THE ARCH

It is believed by some that about ten years after its completion, the world-famous St. Louis Arch, the Gateway to the West, 630 feet of stainless steel in cantilever fashion in Jefferson National Expansion Memorial National Park on the west bank of the Mississippi River, began to affect the weather. Forget El Niño and global warming as causing weather events—it's the Gateway Arch in St. Louis!

For almost forty years, folk beliefs, superstitions, or tales about the power of the Arch to affect weather have been elevated to the status of

legends! In St. Louis folklore, this is a perfect example of how a superstition, with many versions, can be deduced from a legend surrounding
a well-known object. The Arch, alone in its majesty and certainly one
of the architectural marvels of the twentieth century, must have some
"mysterious" power in its "impossible" construction and design. How
else could it be explained except by a "power beyond us?" so the thinking goes.

One version tells us that the Arch was made with the same intent
that scientists of the 1940s used hoping to control weather. Doomsday
weapon research was conducted in the southwestern United States as
an attempt to aid the Allies in ending World War II. But, not known to

the average American, these same scientists attempted to control the weather also, as an aid to troop movement in various parts of Europe. This would be tactically superior to any efforts that the enemy could muster.

It was at this time, so the legend goes, that these scientists conceived the design for the Gateway Arch. Each leg of the Arch, they felt, could push positive and negative ions into the air to create a field that can push storms out of the area. Its structure would be a device to produce an ionic pulse. The Arch was designed to control the weather! Of course, the Midwest of the United States is famous for tornadoes and other kinds of severe storms, including heavy snow and ice. When these storms move with absolute certainty across the country, St. Louis is right in the middle of the imminent havoc. But as they approach St. Louis, for reasons unclear to the layman, they often split, and part of the storm goes north of the city and the other half goes south of the city. The region in the middle does not get any severe weather. And that's where St. Louis is located—directly in the middle! And when they leave the area, these two halves of the storm rejoin and create storm damage in Illinois, Indiana, Ohio, and other states to the east of St. Louis.

This "Arch Effect," the legend tells us, is well known to meteorologists throughout the St. Louis area. And interestingly, they can use the device at their own pleasure to control the weather in the area. If one keeps track of weather phenomena in St. Louis, the legend continues, it will be noticed that the "Arch Effect" does not always work during daylight hours. Why? Because there are too many people in the Arch using the capsules to get to the top in order to see the entire St. Louis area. Those who "control" the Arch as a device use it most often in the evening hours, when there is less risk to people. Using it in this way, those whose fingers control the "effect" will not draw too much attention to their influence.

But it should be noted in the transmission of the legend that the Arch device can be used to actually pull storms into the St. Louis area. True believers swear to occasions when storms were nowhere near the

St. Louis area and forecasters predicted sunny, pleasant skies. And the storms arrived in a way alien to Mother Nature!

So the ability to draw storms, bad weather, weather events—whatever they might be called—are operative in the St. Louis Gateway Arch, the prototypical device. Of course, believers assert, the U.S. government knows of these experiments, conducted since the 1940s, but they continue to cover it up. The engineers and scientists who were involved in the creation of the "wartime" device were moved to other countries to continue their research in controlling weather for a wartime tactic.

Even contractors and construction personnel who assembled the Arch in wondrous fashion were not aware of the secret technology being used. They naively believed, the legend concludes, that they were producing the tallest monument in the United States, which honored St. Louis as the Gateway to the West and the pioneers who settled the manifest destiny of the United States.

It is interesting to note that some versions of the belief in the power of the Arch have a U.S. president controlling the "button," or a terrorist organization infiltrating the "device," or even, historically, when scientists were working on the device in the desert decades ago that the Germans had tried to infiltrate spies into the laboratories. Of course, they were discovered and executed!

So, the Gateway Arch, specific to St. Louis, Missouri, is a device to control weather. Here is an excellent example of a belief, becoming a superstition, becoming a legend, and often it is discovered in the opposite way. "Don't ask me why," is often heard, "but the Arch Effect did it again!"

Whether it's folk medicine, planting, eating, household activities, monuments, or the rites of passage, there are superstitions to cover every aspect. Again, they are informally learned but traditionally practiced and passed on and on and on. They become personal lore that helps us explain the world to ourselves. And apparently if one is a meteorologist in St. Louis, the lore allows us to rain on any parade.

KEEP YOUR LORE ALIVE!

LET ME REPEAT MYSELF: FOLKLORE IS NOT STATIC! IT IS A DYNAMIC PROCESS. It does not live in a vacuum. It means something. It reflects our wishes, desires, hopes, frustrations, aspirations, worries, concerns, fears, even our future.

In the first edition of *Passing It On*, I tried to describe the flowing movement of the oral tradition which is folklore. Through folk vocabulary, folk sayings, rituals, beliefs, stories, rhymes, foods, even graffiti from the St. Louis area, a pattern of our culture was presented. All of it, I hoped, showed what folklore represents for all of us.

And you responded. This new edition includes more of the folklore that I have collected from those who have dug deeply into their memories or reflected on their own daily learning process and perhaps met their parents and grandparents again. After reading the first edition, many understood what folklore, folkways, and folklife means. They related to the importance of preserving it, documenting it, and thinking about it.

But there is more to be collected. What about occupations and their lore? What about the many other ethnic groups in St. Louis? What about urban belief tales? How does the computer contribute to St. Louis lore? Where does the next folk vocabulary come from? How do Baby Boomers, senior citizens, or minorities transmit folklore in the twenty-first century? What does it say about our tomorrows? Collect it or lose it!

There will be more lore to be preserved. For now, I hope you enjoy the texts in this revised edition.

Let me conclude with one final folk text. It is sent to me dozens of times and attributed to Andy Rooney, George Carlin, Mother Theresa, Steve Allen, Jay Leno, and even the late Bob Hardy and Jim White of KMOX (CBS) in St. Louis. No matter the author and no matter that it is not exclusively St. Louis, it still resonates. The proverbial bottom line of folkways is the "people." No matter what the folk group is; no matter how argumentative the meanings of our folk texts may be; all the diverse folk groups will agree with the sentiments.

HOW TO STAY YOUNG

1. Throw out nonessential numbers. This includes age, weight, and height. Let the doctor worry about them. That is why you pay him or her.

2. Keep only cheerful friends. The grouches will pull you down.

3. Keep learning. Learn more about the computer, crafts, gardening, music, whatever. Never let the brain idle, the devil is lurking. And the devil is Alzheimer's.

4. Enjoy the simple things.

5. Laugh often, long, and loud. Laugh until you gasp for breath.

6. The tears will happen. Endure, grieve, and move on. The only person who is with you your entire life is *you*. Be *alive* while you are alive.

7. Surround yourself with what you love, whether it's family, pets, keepsakes, music, plants, hobbies, whatever you want. Your home is your refuge.

8. Cherish your health. If it is good, preserve it. If it is unstable, improve it. If it is beyond what you can improve, get help.

9. Don't take guilt trips. Take a trip to the mall, to the next city, to another country, but *not* to the guilt.

10. Tell the people you love that you love them, at every opportunity.

11. Greet everyone with a kind word. Ask the clerk how her day is going.

12. At the end of the day, ask yourself, *every* day: How Did I Make the World Better Today?

Preserve the memories in your lore, and then pass them on. It's the best legacy.

ABOUT THE AUTHOR

DR. JOHN L. OLDANI—DR. JACK TO HIS STUDENTS—IS A NATIVE OF ST. Louis and the city's unofficial ambassador. With a PhD in American Studies from Saint Louis University, he was a professor for thirty years, primarily at Southern Illinois University at Edwardsville, and visiting professor at the University of Florida, Gainesville, University of California, Berkeley, and University of Zagreb, Croatia. Dr. Jack's passion, study, and mission have been the folklore of St. Louis. He has collected it for decades throughout the region and has taken it with him to other parts of the country, even the world, to validate and verify. Dr. Oldani had a syndicated newspaper column, "American Folksay," and served as the only writer for Johnny Cash's radio program, "American Folklore," producing 550 scripts. He has received numerous teaching awards and was inducted into the Great Professor Hall of Fame. He is also the author of *You Did What in the Ditch? Folklore of the American Quilt* and *Sweetness Preserved, The History of the Crown Candy Kitchen*, a St. Louis icon. He resides in St. Louis with his wife, three children, and their spouses. But his grandchildren, Gemma Oldani, Josie and Ceci Hendrickson, and Charlie Oldani are now his subjects of study and give the greatest meaning to his life and new "research." But after all these years of studying folklore, Dr. Oldani has not discovered the folk cure for baldness and is still searching.

If you have folklore that you would like to share with Dr. Jack, please contact him through his website: stlouisfolklore.com.

INDEX

1904 World's Fair, 105, 115
  food at, 119
Amighetti's, 116
Anheuser-Busch, 111, 114
Arena, 55
Arnold, Missouri, 56, 149
Art Hill, 55,
autograph books, 12-25
Ballwin, 126
Barnhart, 57
Bausch, Patty, 71
Bender, John, 67
Bergman, Ann, 96
Bevo Mill, 111, 140
Billiken Company of Chicago, 67
Billiken, 67-68
birthmark, xiii, 70, 72
Bisesi, Judy, 98
Bissell's Point, 136
Bissinger's, 122
black cats, xiii, xviii, 69, 80
bread, xiv, 79, 132-135
Braun, Betty Wickes, 170
Buck, Jack, 76
Budweiser, 54-55, 149
Burnes, Bob, 14
Busch Stadium, 57
Carl's Hamburgers, 122
caul, xiii, 72
Cervantes, Mayor Alfonso, 149
Cherokee Street, 57
Christmas, 83-84, 91-94, 98, 102-103, 115,
  133-134, 140-141, 143-145, 175
Christmas Spider Legend, 144-145
Clayton, 149
Concordia Seminary, 136

Conway, Mayor James, 149
Cook, Jim, 103
Cook, Pat, 103
Crab Rangoon, 115
Croatia (Croatian), xiii, 123-124, 130-132
Crown Candy Kitchen, 117, 122
Crystal City, 55
Dad's Cookie Company, 116-117
Dannehold, Sandra, 98, 100
Deachan, Kathy Tepe, 79-80
Dowd, James F. (Jim), III, 78
Drewes, Ted, 5, 55, 57, 112-113
Duomo, (Milan, Italy), 15, 134
Dutchtown, 4, 57, 136-137
Easter Sunday, 6, 84, 88-89, 102-104, 115,
  129, 134, 157
Ellis Island, xiii
Ethnic folklore, 123-135. See also individual
  ethnicities.
Falstaff, 45, 55
family traditions, 96-98
Famous-Barr, 121, 148-149
Festus, 55
"Fishbowl," 121
Fitz's Root Beer, 119-120
flea market, 142
foods, 105-122. See also individual foods.
  German, 142-143
freckles, cure for, xiv, 126
French Onion Soup, 121-122
garlic, xiv, 126, 129, 132
Gassel, Betty, 104
Gateway Arch, 54
  power of, with weather, 176-179
German folklore, 136-145
Gitto, Charlie, 106

Gooey Butter Cake, 118
"Grand Leader," 55
graffiti, 146-164
    Internet graffiti, 151
griot, xiii, 167
Gunn, Billy, 67
Gus' Pretzels, 114-115
Halloween, xv, 52, 92, 94
hat (on a bed), xiii, 97
Highlands, 55
Hill, The, 15, 106, 113, 116, 121, 123
Huber, Darlene, 102
Hyde Park, 136
Imo, Ed, 107-108
Imo's Pizza, 55, 107-108
Imperial, 56
Intagliata, Christine, 165-166
Intagliata, Ed, 165-166
Intagliata family, 165-175
Intagliata, Jenni, 170
Intagliata, Juanita, 171
Intagliata, Marie (Mimi), 165-166
Intagliata, Rosemary Wickes, 165-166
Intagliata, Russell, 165
Italian folklore, 127-129
Jewish folklore, 124-127
jokes, 51-58
Keller, Nellie, 71
Kirkwood, 57
Ladue, 56-58
Lakamp, Kevin, 79
Lake of the Ozarks, 55
"Lower Affton," 55
Malcolm Bliss, 162-163
Mallinckrodt, 136
Mama Campisi's Restaurant, 106
Maull, Louis, 110
Maull's Barbecue Sauce, 110-111
Mayfair Hotel, 111-112
Mayflower Prosperity Sandwich, 121

Miller, Terry, 118
medicine, folk, 82, 99, 118, 171, 179
    Italian, 128-129
    Jewish, 126
    Slavic, 131-132
momisms, 59-66
moon, 72
    full, xiv, 100, 129, 132
    ring around, xiv
Moses, D. James (Jim), 101
Murphy, Juanita, 97
National Food Stores, 148
New Year's Day, 83-86, 92, 140, 143
O.T. Hodge's, 122
Pasta House, 56
pelinkovac, xiii, 131
Pestalozzi Street, 55
Phil the Gorilla, 29, 42
Pink Sisters, 55
pork steaks, 109
potatoes, xiv, 61, 82, 143
potica, xiv, 134-135
Powell, Carol, 89
predictions, folk, 69, 99
Pretz, Florence, 67
Red Hot Riplets, 117-118
Red Rover, xiii
Renard the Fox, 111
rhymes
    counting-out rhymes, 26-32
    insults, 39-43
    hand clapping, 43-47
    jump-rope, 32-39
    parodies, 47-50
riddles, 51-58
Rigazzi's Restaurant, 121
River des Peres, 56
Roberts Mayfair Hotel, 111-112
Rosh Hashanah, 84
Saint Louis University, 67-68

Saint Louis Zoo, 29, 81, 169
St. Martin's Day, 140-142
St. Paul Sandwich, 108-109
sayings, folk, 99
   German, 139
   Italian, 127
   Jewish, 124-125
   Slavic, 130-131
Schnucks, 148
Silver Dollar City, 55
Slavic (Croatian) folklore, 130-132
Slay, Mayor Francis, 149
Slinger, 110
songs, folk, xiii, xvi, 167
superstitions, 67-82
   childhood, 70-72
   marriage, 73-76
   death, 76-78
   German, 140
Tepe, Henry A., 79
Tepe, Mary, 79

Thanksgiving, 9, 78, 84, 89-90, 98, 143
Toasted Ravioli, 54-55, 106, 119
Tucker, Mayor Raymond, 149
umbrellas (in the house), xiii, 97
Valentine's Day, 84, 86-88
Veiled Prophet, 15, 56
vocabulary, folk, 3-11
   family, 95-96
   German, 137-138
   Jewish, 126
Volpi's, 121
Wal-Mart, 56
Warren, Betty Intagliata, 167, 172
Warren, Marty, 138
weather, 100-104
   Arch, 176-179
Wickes, George, 165, 170
Wickes, Norine, 168, 170
Woofie's, 122
World's Fair Bird Cage, 81, 119